ALONE

with God

A Guide for Personal Retreats

✳

Ron DelBene
with Herb & Mary Montgomery

UPPER
ROOM BOOKS
NASHVILLE

Cover Design by Bruce Gore (Nashville).
First Printing: September 1992 (7).
Library of Congress Catalog Number: 92-80944.
ISBN: 0-8358-0668-5.
Printed in The United States of America.

To my father and mother

Also by the Authors

Christmas Remembered
From the Heart

The Into the Light Collection
Into the Light
When I'm Alone
Near Life's End
A Time to Mourn (also on cassette)
Study Guide

The Times of Change, Times of Challenge Series
When You Are Getting Married
When Your Child Is Baptized
When You Are Facing Surgery
When an Aging Loved One Needs Care
When You Are Facing a Decision
When You Are Living with an Illness That Is Not Your Own

The Breath of Life Series
The Breath of Life
The Hunger of the Heart
Alone with God

C O N T E N T S

P R E F A C E

Ron DelBene and I met in the late sixties while working at a publishing house in Minneapolis where he was the national consultant in religion and I was an editor. Our families were young then, so we had common interests both on and off the job, but we did not begin our writing collaboration until years later. By then a bond of friendship was formed even though both of us had made career changes. I left publishing but stayed in Minnesota where Mary and I pursued careers as professional writers. Ron and his family moved to Florida where he developed a ministry in spiritual direction and was ordained.

In 1980 Ron was teaching a form of prayer that was new to me and so intriguing that I encouraged him to write a book about it. He agreed on the condition that I work with him, and so began a collaboration that has continued into the nineties. Ron's first book, *The Breath of Life: A Simple Way to Pray*, was originally published in 1981. Some ten years later, it needed updating along with the two books that promptly followed publication of his first one: *Hunger of the Heart* and *Alone with God*. We invited Mary to join us in revising these three editions that Upper Room Books now publishes as the *Breath of Life Series*.

Over the years of watching Ron move away from the business world to be ordained and go on to serve as pastor and spiritual director, I have been impressed by his commitment to practice what he counsels others to do. Though he is quick to admit that preaching spiritual discipline comes easier than practicing it, he routinely sets aside time to be alone with God. The breath prayer, which is an integral part of his spiritual life, is something he has been using for more than thirty years.

9

For well over a decade, Ron has encouraged those who come to him seeking spiritual direction to keep a journal of their experiences. These deeply-felt personal writings reflect some aspects of what happens when we invite God to enter more fully into our life. Numerous journal entries are included in this book, and all are used with permission of the people who wrote them. Their hope is that others who are trying to draw closer to God will benefit from their experiences. The entries appear as they were written, but in the interest of privacy, names and certain identifying details have been changed.

Each of Ron's books speaks to readers in a gentle, caring way, never asking others to do what he hasn't done himself. His invitation to others to take responsibility for their spiritual growth is sincere and loving. I hope that this new edition of *Alone with God* will inspire you on your spiritual journey.

HERB MONTGOMERY

C H A P T E R   1

Alonetime

Beginnings

A group of us were sitting around a fireplace quietly sharing thoughts about the retreat for which we had gathered. Although we arrived at the retreat as strangers, a feeling of warmth and support had developed among us. This created the trust we needed to allow others into our private thoughts.

Susan was the first to speak up. A wife and mother of a teenage son, she said, "It's amazing that I'd be afraid to be alone with God!" I knew it had been hard for Susan (as it was for the others) to get away for this retreat. Her admission changed the level of our conversation, bringing forth deeper feelings about what it is like to reach out to God on our own.

Casey, a young lawyer active in community affairs, echoed Susan's concerns. "Often I think I want to take some time just to be alone with God," he said, "but then I immediately wonder, What would I do?"

The conversation that evening confirmed what I had been hearing through the years in retreats I had been giving all across the United States as well as in private spiritual direction sessions. That is, *many of us find it extremely difficult to be alone with God because we are not sure what to do and have no idea what to expect.*

Uncertainty is not something we like to admit, but it does exist and is a barrier that anyone seriously concerned about personal spiritual growth must break through. This book is my response to the people who want to be alone with God and are at a loss as to what to do about it. Martha, for example, is a middle-aged homemaker living in a small Southern town. "I have no one to direct me in my alonetime," she told me. "If only there were someone nearby, or something to guide me."

Although Bradley is a city dweller, he expressed much the same sentiment as Martha when he said, "Even though there are a lot of resources where I live, there are times when I'd like to just take my Bible and go off for a couple of hours or even a day—in the woods, at the beach, or just in the church. But I'd feel foolish. I need some direction."

It used to be that people wanted to be alone with God in some quiet setting exclusively for what we called "spiritual reasons." While these spiritual reasons still exist, in more recent times there has been an increased awareness of the need for physical, mental, and emotional renewal as well. One Midwestern college recognized this need to the extent that it will not grant a degree to anyone who has not completed at least one course whose purpose is to help students understand their need for self re-creation.

Many of the hurried, hassled people I counsel are concerned about their inability to slow down; they are unable to reflect, exercise, improve their diet, or pay attention to their environment. Those who decide to spend a little time alone with God soon realize it is foolish to try to "get right" with God without considering their whole life and the need to correct *whatever* is out of balance. They are yearning to put not only one room but their entire house in order. I believe this is best done when we are attentive to God's power in our lives. The place to begin is a setting where we can be alone with God and admit our fears and deepest yearnings. Then we will recognize that God's power and Spirit call us to be whole people. Jesus will say to us as he so often said to his followers, "Do not be afraid."

As we begin to look at this venture, it is important to realize that at least part of our hesitancy is based on messages that say being alone and being lonely are the same experience. Advertising, for example, plays on the idea that if we use the right toothpaste, drink the right cola, and wear the right clothes, we will have lots of friends and be neither alone nor lonely. Such commercial messages may sell products, but they create misconceptions. Being alone and being lonely are not the same. While it is true that we may be lonely when we are alone, we can experience that same isolation in a crowd—and it can happen even though we are wearing trendy clothing and driving the right van. Lonely is what we feel: an emotion, an inner experience. Alone is what we are: a physical placement, an outer condition.

As it relates to being alone with God, I consider the word "alone" to involve placing ourselves in a setting where we are free of distractions and better able to focus on God. In this sense, being alone is a positive experience; it is an opportunity to see the depth of ourselves. We have all known people who can put on a happy face whenever they feel the situation calls for it. Such people are playing a part and wearing a mask. When we are alone with God, we can take off our mask and reveal on the outside what we are feeling on the inside. This is a positive step toward becoming who God is calling us to be.

Being alone with God will not dispel all lonely feelings, and the results of our spiritual seeking may not be immediate. But in my work as a spiritual director I have seen that over time God fills us with the inner strength we need to seek worthwhile relationships, build friendships, and involve ourselves in activities that give a feeling of wholeness. Eventually such purposeful involvement leaves us with little time for feeling lonely.

Attentiveness

Did you ever say something to your boss, friend, spouse, or child and feel as if you were talking to a brick wall? If so, you knew that that person was not paying attention to what you had to say. There was talk but no communication. It is somewhat the same when God speaks to us either directly or through others, and we fail to pay attention. How many times have we missed opportunities of ministry or service because we were not attentive? When we complain about not feeling God's presence, perhaps we are like the unlistening wall that we find so infuriating in our relationships.

Being attentive is key to spending time alone with God. Although we can be attentive right at home, many people find other surroundings more conducive to reflection and prayer. Getting away from our everyday environment and activities tends to put us in a heightened state and we look and listen with greater awareness. When we are truly attentive, we are more likely to discern what we must do to be more in touch with God and to understand God's purpose for us.

Silence: An Enemy or a Friend?

Did you ever get the silent treatment as a child or as an adult? It is a treatment often used by people who want to punish us. In such a circumstance, silence is something we dread; silence, as well as the person who uses it as a weapon, becomes the enemy. In other circumstances, silence is equated with doing nothing, with lack of productivity, and sometimes even with evil. If purposeful quiet is viewed negatively, learning to be silent (still) in God's presence may be very difficult, as it was for Mike. An over-scheduled dentist, his days were filled with nonstop activity both in and out of the office. At age thirty-six, he came to the Hermitage, a small guest residence on our property where people came to reflect and pray under my guidance. There, Mike planned to spend four days in solitude. After the first evening without the usual company of radio, TV, or people with whom he might talk, he made this journal entry:

> Here I am. For nearly four months, I've been looking forward to coming here and having some time alone with God, but I'm suddenly filled with a great deal of apprehension. What will I do? I realize now that I'm a doer, and here all I have to do is be. I'm not a be-er. (But I'd love a beer!)
> I'm really afraid . . . .

Why would a grown man be apprehensive about spending four days in silence, solitude, and prayer? Because, as a doer, Mike saw silence as unproductive. Consequently, he felt powerless. What was expected of him? He did not know. Deep down it was a control issue; he wanted to be in control rather than giving over his power—his control—to God. Perhaps deep down Mike was afraid because he knew he was being called to greater wholeness, and that would bring about change in his life.

Mike's word play on be-er and beer points up how, when we face a difficult situation regarding growth, spiritual or otherwise, we often seek some diversion. Food, drink, humor, music, sports, clothes, and sometimes even religion are used to ignore paying attention to where God is calling us.

As a child growing up in Ohio, I often went to a lake cottage with my parents. My father was an attorney and my mother a nurse. For them, the cottage setting was wonderful because there was no phone, no TV, no mail, and a radio that was to be turned on only for emergency weather reports. The place seemed dull to me, especially for the first few hours, but then I found ways to entertain myself. Since then the "laketime" of my youth has become a pleasant memory, because today I often find my life run by the telephone and the mail. Now I welcome the silence I did not appreciate as a child. Instead of silence being an enemy, it has become a friend.

To respect the true value of silence, we need only recall those moments when we have been touched in soundless but wondrous ways. Rocking a child to sleep, quietly stroking a cherished pet, the presence of a dear friend—each is a comforting experience that requires no words. Our presence alone speaks to child, pet, and friend alike. Likewise, God's presence speaks to us when we are attentive and ready to hear. But in the busyness of our lives, it is all too easy to ignore our spiritual listening ability.

I remember my days as a religious education consultant when I traveled the crowded freeways morning and night and shuttled back and forth across the U.S. by plane. It seemed as if I was never away from noise. Then one summer we took a family vacation in Canada's Sibley Provincial Park on the north side of Lake Superior. I had forgotten quiet and what it can mean. But quiet was there. Along with sky blues and earth greens, my senses were refreshed and open to "hearing the silence." Hiking along a nature trail, I recognized how the pace of the business world and the clamor of city living can deaden our capacity to listen for and recognize what is sacred.

What about you? Are you ready to let go of some of the busyness and pressures of your life and rediscover silence? You can begin with as few as two hours and—when you are ready for it—build up to a weekend. Come, my friend, I invite you to journey a little further spiritually by taking time to be alone with God.

Finding Space

We each have a need to define and defend our space. This is apparent even in young children who wall off an area with blocks or chairs and throw tantrums if anyone intrudes. They turn a cardboard box into a house that no one may enter unless invited. Older children hang signs on their bedroom doors—signs that range from Private, Keep Out to Disaster Zone or Enter at Your Own Risk.

As adults, we lay claim to some part of the place in which we live. It may be a corner of a bedroom, a darkroom, a sewing room, a workbench area of the basement, or even a shed in the backyard. At the very least, we set aside a certain chair. Other family members tend to respect this staking out of territory because they recognize their need to do the same. The need for our own space applies to our spiritual lives as well. We want a place to go where we can be alone with God, and we need the assurance from others that that place will be respected. Whether the space is large or small does not matter. What is important is knowing that the space is ours when we want or need it.

For our time alone with God, we want an environment that is peaceful and conducive to reflection. Most people find it extremely difficult to feel peaceful and reflective when the surroundings are jarring to their senses. If you do not have a suitable space, or one that can be easily adapted to your purposes, why not look first to your church building and see whether there might already be a space that suits your needs?

More and more churches are setting aside places for individuals seeking quiet time for reflection and meditation. One church I visited transformed a little used storage area into a retreat room. The floor was carpeted, attractive artwork hung on the walls, and a small altar served as a focal point. A desk and a comfortable chair were provided for reading and writing, and a cot stood along one wall for anyone needing rest. People who want to use the room make a reservation by calling the church office and then stop by at the appointed time to pick up the key.

Another church has a similar arrangement, but also provides an under-the-counter refrigerator so that people who want to stay all day, or through mealtime, have a place to store food.

A somewhat different approach is offered by a church that has a "still place" with a small library of inspirational tapes and books people may listen to or read.

Yet another church uses a thematic approach, basing the decor of the meditation space on scripture. Church members designed and painted a large burning bush on one wall. The bush is the focal point of the room that is referred to as "holy ground."

Using a room within their local church is especially convenient for people who do not like to be alone without someone nearby. If your church does not have a private prayer room, discuss the idea with others and see whether it is something to pursue.

Your home is, of course, the next place to consider. Although very few of us can reserve an entire room for our spiritual pursuits, most of us can set aside some part of our house or apartment where we can be alone and undisturbed for a time. Unfortunately, there are drawbacks to making even a two-hour retreat at home. In everyday surroundings, we tend to think and act in familiar ways and are less open to new possibilities. Being aware of this is helpful when we commit ourselves to spending time alone with God at home. To avoid interruptions and distractions, silence the doorbell with a note such as "Do not disturb until (time)" and quiet the phone by either unplugging it, connecting it to an answering machine, or putting it on the softest ring and muffling the sound with pillows.

If you prefer being alone with God in nature, consider a park, a beach, a forest, the desert, or other place of your choice. It is important that you feel physically secure in the setting and that you have the level of privacy you find necessary.

Alone time can also be combined with a day or two of rest and recreation. Expenses can be kept to a minimum by renting a cabin during the off season. Large hotel and motel complexes often have weekend specials that may or may not be well advertised. By making a few phone calls, you can find out if such special rates are offered and what they include. Auto clubs and organizations such as AARP may qualify members for an additional discount. In some cities, weekend rates are as little as one-half the usual charge, and the use of a pool or other athletic facility is often included at no extra fee. Other possibilities include a retreat center, a church camp, a chapel, or a gazebo in the backyard.

The place you choose is not important. What matters is that it affords you the peace and privacy necessary for reflection and prayer. If you are a bit anxious or apprehensive about this spiritual venture, regard it as a sign that you are about to begin something significant.

What You Need and What You Do

After you have decided where you are going to spend your time alone with God, you will need certain items. The following checklist includes items that are essential and others that are optional. If you plan to make a personal retreat of this type on a regular basis, you might want to store these items in a single container. I know one woman who keeps everything ready in a wicker basket. All she has to do is pick up her basket and head for her favorite location, a bench in a nearby park that is quiet and safe. There she spends two hours alone with God every other weekend.

Here are items to take, along with this book:

____ A Bible. Even though your copy of *Alone With God* includes the necessary scripture for each session, it is good to have your own Bible. (When people ask which translation is best, I recommend they go to a bookstore and read favorite passages from several translations and select one they favor. Some Bibles have study aids, cross-references, and dictionaries of biblical terms.)

____ Writing paper. A spiral-bound or loose-leaf notebook is needed for keeping notes.

____ Drawing paper if you draw or sketch to express yourself.

____ Crayons, sketch pencils, chalks, or paints if these are your means of expression.

____ Two pens or pencils, in case one breaks or goes dry.

____ A timer or a clock that includes an alarm.

Here are optional items that many people find useful in creating a comfortable, prayerful environment:

____ A cross or crucifix.

____ A picture of Jesus or an icon. ("Icon" is the Greek word for "image" used in Genesis 1:26, which says we are created in God's image. The word has continued to be used in the Christian tradition of the East to refer to pictures of Jesus, his mother Mary, and holy men and women throughout Christian history. We can be encouraged on our spiritual path by following the examples of these faithful people of God.)

____ A flower or flowers.

____ A candle. A votive candle in a glass is safest in the event you fall asleep with the candle burning.

____ Incense.

____ A cushion or blanket.

____ A lightweight folding chair.

____ Water or juice.

____ Fruit or other light snack.

Set a Time

Steve, an ordained man who had been coming to me for spiritual direction, complained that he was having trouble finding time to sit quietly and pray. One Monday morning when we met, he showed me his appointment calendar. Pointing to the filled page, he said, "Look here," and began reading off what he had to do, hour by hour.

Finally I broke in and asked, "What are you doing at eleven on Wednesday or Thursday?"

"I'm busy Wednesday," he said, "but I've got the hour open on Thursday."

"Why not write down prayer for that time slot?" My suggestion caught him by surprise, but he picked up on it. After that I did not see him for a couple of weeks. The next time we met he told me he had turned down a call for lunch at eleven on that particular Thursday and kept his time commitment to himself. Like so many I meet who are busy from morning until night, Steve was waiting to serve his own needs during what I call the twenty-fifth hour—the hour that never arrives.

What about you? Are you also waiting for the twenty-fifth hour to give more attention to your spiritual life? If so, why not make an appointment with yourself? Set a time to put aside your regular activities and commit yourself to being alone with God. If this is a new experience for you, set a realistic goal. In the beginning, just *taking* the time is more important than the amount of time you spend.

For first-time users of this book, I recommend setting aside at least one hour, but not more than two. On the other hand, if you are already disciplining yourself to pray, meditate, or read scripture on a regular basis, you may be ready to set aside as many as four hours, or even plan an entire weekend. If you like to schedule ahead, you will notice that there are twelve sessions in the book for a once-a-month time alone with God.

Follow the Plan

The sessions outlined in Part II are designed for a two-hour period and divided into a number of activities, each of which has a recommended time. If your schedule is tight, use a timer so that you do not stay too long on any one activity.

Which session should I do first? Although it is recommended that you do the sessions in sequence, each one is self-contained so you can rearrange the sequence to suit your needs and interests. For example, if you are troubled about forgiving or being forgiven, turn to the "Seeking Forgiveness" session and begin there. Remember that your time alone with God is meant to be a spiritually rewarding experience. Plunge into whatever topic is of most importance to you *at this time.* By doing so you are likely to resolve the issue, or at least get a new perspective on it.

What do I do if I have only one hour? Give each of the activities in the two-hour session you have selected one-half the time suggested, or do half the session now and half later.

Many of the suggestions can be picked up on at a later time. For example, you might find a few free minutes to complete the activity after your evening meal, when you would otherwise watch TV, or just before bedtime.

Can anything go wrong? Not really. Of course you might be interrupted for some unforeseen reason. If that happens, reschedule the time and begin again. It is not uncommon to fall asleep and wake up feeling guilty when you discover how time has slipped away.

Generally when I set aside a twenty-four-hour period, I go in the evening and stay until late the next afternoon. That allows for a good sleep and a fresh start in the morning. Once I began around four-thirty in the afternoon. My day had been hectic, so I lay down to rest a bit. I woke up at nine that evening, ate something, and then returned to my schedule. While reflecting on scripture, I fell asleep again and did not wake up until the next morning! In my early days as a spiritual director I would have felt very guilty, but at that point I was experienced enough to realize that God understands our needs better than we do. On that day my need was for sleep, and God provided it. Though I must admit I felt rather sheepish when I told my wife Eleanor what had happened.

If you fall asleep while praying, consider it a clue. Are you working under too much pressure? Do you need to slow your pace? Do you need to look for ways to rest yourself physically as well as mentally?

Be aware that it is not unusual to cry during a session that has deep personal meaning. The tears may result from being unburdened or they may be a part of the wonder and joy that come from being forgiven and accepted just as you are. (If this is your experience, you may find it helpful to read about the gift of tears in Chapter 9 of *The Breath of Life: Discovering Your Breath Prayer*.)

The Plan

When people pursue being alone with God, they generally prefer various activities of short duration rather than one lengthy reflection. Thus the plan I developed divides the two hours into ten activities. *The time allotted for each activity is a guideline that can be changed to suit your needs.* For example, if your life is hectic, you might double the time spent in silence and shorten the time spent on reading the scripture selection. Before making changes, go through at least one two-hour period as outlined. Then adapt the schedule if you need to do so.

1. *Create the Environment* (5 minutes) Prepare the space and make yourself comfortable. This includes anything from unplugging the phone at home to putting out a Do Not Disturb sign in a motel. You may want to arrange some flowers, light a candle, open your Bible, get comfortable in a chair.

2. *Open with Prayer* Begin with prayer to set the mood and theme of the session. A prayer is included in each section. Additional prayers from which to choose are in Part Three.

3. *Be Still* (10 minutes) Do whatever helps you wind down and clear your mind. Some people find that breathing deeply three or four times and relaxing the shoulders is a good way to get comfortable and be silent. Close your eyes and listen as you settle into being alone with God. Other people find that doing a little body movement (gentle stretching, dancing, exercising) helps them relax and become still. If you find yourself daydreaming or distracted, try a short prayer to bring you back into focus—perhaps "Jesus, let me feel your presence," or "O God, lead me into peace." Saying the Lord's Prayer or a favorite line from a hymn or psalm serves the same purpose. Distractions are normal and nothing to worry about. When they occur, simply return to your short prayer and refocus your attention.

4. *Read and Reflect on Scripture* (25 minutes) Each session includes the scripture to be read. If you prefer, you may read it from your own Bible. I suggest that you read it aloud to yourself because there is power in the spoken word. At first you may feel awkward, but the feeling is temporary. As you read, let God's Spirit lead you. There is no need to get through the reading quickly. Let any meaningful word or line or image do what it will. A prayer or a memory or another thought about God may be triggered. Pray that prayer, pursue that memory or thought. If you feel the urge to do so, write something down, make a sketch, or create a collage.

Read the same selection over and over with the awareness that God is present. If the first or second reading does not strike a chord, continue rereading the passage until the time is up. Do this even if the repetition is tiresome. Before your time alone is over, the reading will have an impact on you.

Many express their concern about God being referred to with masculine nouns and pronouns. Although churches and church groups are suggesting a range of alternatives, currently there is no universal solution. I have selected scripture mainly from the New Revised Standard Version (NRSV), a familiar and popular translation. During this transitional time, I use the word "God" in most of my writing, but on occasion I also use the masculine "Lord." I try to include as few masculine pronouns as possible, but admit that I am a writer caught in the middle. I sincerely hope those of you who want to keep things just as they are and those of you who want inclusive language appreciate my dilemma and will be understanding.

5. *Another Dimension* (15 minutes) I have prepared a reflection to provide another dimension to the scripture reading. This is a brief meditation that presents another view of the passage, or enables you to see an aspect of the story you may not have considered before.

6. *Break/Rest/Body Movement* (15 minutes) We all need time for things to settle in, so take a break. If possible, get outside and breathe deeply as you walk or stretch. Have some water or juice or a piece of fruit. If you feel drowsy, take a nap.

7. *Inner Dimension* (30 minutes) This period is for inner reflection and is a task designed to help you clarify God's action in your life. The inner dimension sections vary in content but generally require using your notebook or art materials. Depending on how freely you express yourself, you may feel that too much or too little time has been allotted. Extend or shorten the time accordingly. If you finish quickly, look back over what you have expressed, allowing God's Spirit to lead you to other insight.

8. *Prayer of Response* (10 minutes) Pray in your own style, or use a prayer from Part III. The time may seem long if you are new to prayer or have never prayed for more than a few seconds at a time. Simply speak to God, honestly and directly.

9. *Reflection* (10 minutes) This is a time to review what you have been doing during your alone time. People report various experiences: a discovery of how to pray, an insight regarding scripture, a desire to change a particular behavior, an emotional awakening.

10. *Close with Prayer* Closing prayers that relate to the themes are included. You may use your own prayer or choose one from Part III.

Although a retreat of even so brief a time as two hours can serve several functions, the main purpose is to provide the opportunity to move closer to God, the source of all love. Any nervousness or anxiety you feel during or after the session could indicate that you are not yet comfortable with this new experience, or that your relationship with God needs more attention than you have been giving it.

CHAPTER 4

How to Recognize Spiritual Growth

"Where am I on the spiritual path?" people ask. "How do I know if I am growing?" Spiritual growth tends to be less visible than physical growth, but that does not make it any less real. If we are working and sharing with a group of caring people or with a spiritual director, we may get some indication as to how we are progressing. Although more and more people have a spiritual guide or friend to help them, many must find some way to measure progress on their own. To this end, a journal is a helpful tool.

Using a Journal

Often people who come to my conferences or meet with me privately admit they are in a state of confusion. As soon as they have shared their ideas they say, "Just getting it out has cleared up so much." Keeping a journal serves somewhat the same function. Expressing your thoughts and feelings in some external form—written or drawn—gives you a record that helps keep important moments alive and provides benchmarks against which to chart your spiritual development. Although a journal is obviously a subjective yardstick, it is one of the best ways we have to measure spiritual growth. If you have tried keeping a journal and failed, try again. The following are six ways of journaling that can give you the sort of information you need to recognize the spiritual changes taking place within you:

1. *Random Note-taking*

A doctor I know keeps a small notebook in his jacket pocket at all times. Whenever something happens that he believes is potentially important in his spiritual development, he makes a note of it. The notes would not make sense to anyone but the doctor. If in your own life you feel there is special meaning in the new ideas, insights, and remembrances generated by anything from the change of seasons to a visit to the old hometown, consider keeping a journal of random notes. Date the entries and write down as much or as little as necessary for the notes to make sense to you. A filled notebook may include everything from sayings you want to remember to comments on a book you read.

2. *Dream Recording*

In keeping notes about your dreams, set up a code that indicates whether the events recorded came from day dreams or night dreams. Both are important. Although we all dream several times every night, some people find it difficult to recall their sleep dreams. If you are such a person, put a pencil and pad beside your bed, and when you wake up right after having a dream, record it then. Otherwise record what you can remember immediately upon awakening in the morning. If you cannot remember a dream, try to capture a word, feeling, or image that comes to you. Write it down, draw it, or speak it into a tape recorder. One problem with tapes, however, is that they are harder to review than notebooks. With tapes you have to listen to everything, which takes more time than skimming notes.

Scripture is filled with dream events. Jacob's dream and Joseph's interpretation of dreams are examples from the Hebrew Scripture, commonly called the Old Testament. Should we read books on the subject and try to interpret our own dreams? Many books are available, but I think initially it is more important to record both day dreams and night dreams than it is to interpret them. Recognizing dream patterns does not necessarily require specialized knowledge of symbols or psychology. For example, if you daydream constantly about leaving a job, it may be that you are unhappy in some aspect of your life and should try to identify that unhappiness and then consider making necessary changes. If you are interested in dreams, you might want to begin reading about them. But first I urge you to keep a dream journal or make notes about them in a random journal.

3. Dialogue Journaling *some of this~*

~Do you often find~ yourself thinking one thing and feeling another? If so, you would probably find it helpful to keep a journal in which you describe the dialogue that goes on between your thinking self and your feeling self. How does what you think differ from what you feel? Do you think of God as a judge, but feel God must be something more than that? Do you think you are quite intelligent about religious matters, but feel you are practicing your faith at the grade-school level? Do you think you should leave your church, but feel it is so much a part of your heritage that you could never change?

Some people question where the internal dialogue comes from and can argue at length about the conscious and the unconscious, good and evil, God and self. Frankly, that seems to me to be an avoidance of the gift of dialoguing that God has given us to help clarify who we are spiritually and what we should be doing.

Besides dialoguing with ourselves, we can dialogue with others, including people in scripture. What a script we could write dialoguing with a loved one who is now dead, but to whom we have things to say that went unsaid. What a script we could write based on Luke 21 if we imagined ourselves walking on the way to Emmaus and suddenly having Jesus at our side. Consider dialoguing as one more good way of committing thoughts to your journal. Many people find it helpful to write dialogue in play form, using names to indicate the speakers. Your characters could be *Thinking Self* and *Feeling Self* or (*Another Person*) and *Me*.

4. *Reflecting* *PRIMARILY THIS TYPE of reflective*

Writing in a journal after reflecting on your day or on an event is another way to evaluate changes taking place in your spiritual life. At the close of the day, recall and reflect on the experiences. This is very much like keeping a diary, the main difference being that in this type of journaling you look for events that have particular significance. (For more about this type of journal keeping, read Chapter 12, "A Journal for Reflection," in *The Breath of Life: Discovering Your Breath Prayer.*)

5. *Outlining Discovery Tasks*

This form of journaling is like a school assignment in that you do a particular activity in the hope of discovering all you can about any subject that bears on your spiritual life. For example, you might find yourself at an impasse because you can no longer accept your earlier idea that God is an old judge in the sky. You could use a journal to record religious impressions from childhood that contributed to the concept: sermons, Sunday School papers, religious art, your parents' presentation of God. How do you presently feel about that concept of God? What do you really believe about God at this point in your life?

When working on a discovery task, you look to the past to help clarify the present and make living in the future more satisfying. If an issue is especially serious, your journal may become quite detailed before you feel the matter is satisfactorily resolved. Often in this form of journaling you get at the subject best by working from the present to the past, rather like peeling an artichoke layer by layer to reach the heart.

6. *Creating Artwork*

Drawing, sketching, painting, and collage making are also ways of journaling. Dating the artwork makes it easy to look back and see if patterns are developing. Throughout the sessions there are opportunities to use a journal in all six of the ways mentioned. Of course you do not have to limit your journaling to alone time with God. If you have never kept a journal before, begin during one of the sessions and then try to set aside five or ten minutes each day to make an entry. Most people find that one journaling approach suits them better than another. Experiment as you go along, and do not give up too soon.

How long is a good trial time for journaling? If you are serious about your spiritual development, journal entries over a six-week period will probably reveal changes that indicate you are growing—growing more prayerful, more disciplined, and more concerned, not only about yourself but about others as well. Looking back at your early entries is likely to make you smile as you realize that although you still have shortcomings, you are a growing, developing person.

Alone with God

This portion of the book contains twelve self-directed retreats. They are presented in individual two-hour sessions, which can be combined to create extended retreat periods of four, six, eight, or more hours. Although the sessions are arranged and numbered for ease of use, they are self-contained and may be used in any order. If you put several sessions together, you may want to take a short break between them or move directly to a time of stillness. As you become more familiar with your time alone, you will probably make some adaptations in the timing.

Session Format

Create the Environment	5 minutes
Open with Prayer	
Be Still	10 minutes
Read and Reflect on Scripture	25 minutes
Another Dimension	15 minutes
Break/Rest/Body Movement	15 minutes
Inner Dimension	30 minutes
Prayer of Response	10 minutes
Reflection	10 minutes
Close with Prayer	
Total	2 hours

Our Many Faces

And when he saw him, he was moved with pity.

✳

Create the Environment (5 minutes)

Take a few minutes to create a comfortable environment for your time alone with God. What you do depends on whether you are indoors or out, at home or away. If you are inside, do whatever is necessary to avoid being interrupted by the telephone or the doorbell. Get comfortable within your space by turning away from anything distracting and by setting up whatever will help you get into a proper frame of mind. You may want to open your Bible and place it within easy reach next to some flowers or a candle.

Will a picture of Jesus, a cross, a crucifix, or an icon help make you more aware of God's presence? If so, place the item near the Bible or wherever you can easily look at it without being distracted. Have at hand everything you may need: notebook, drawing paper, pens, pencils, art materials.

The objective is to be settled before going further.

Open with Prayer

I give you thanks, O God, my Creator. I believe that you love me and call me by name. You know my face as well as my innermost thoughts. May I become more aware of your love today as I am alone with you. May I feel your presence and move closer to seeing you face to face. I pray as your child. *Amen.*

Be Still (10 minutes, set timer)

The purpose of these ten minutes is to relax the body and prepare the mind and heart to become more attentive as you enter into a special time alone with God. Some people do this by sitting quietly, while others find that gentle body movement is helpful. Often when we begin, our minds are cluttered and we feel distracted. Do not fight your thoughts or focus long on those that come to mind. Instead, breathe deeply and evenly as you reflect on scripture. Use a short prayer or this scripture (Psalm 139:23) as a touchstone, and come back to it over and over as you remain silent:

SEARCH ME, O GOD, AND KNOW MY HEART.

Read and Reflect on Scripture (25 minutes, set timer)

The story for this session (Luke 10:30-35) is that of the Good Samaritan. Read the story over and over. You may like to read it quietly and then again out loud. There is great power in the spoken word, even when it is your voice and you are the audience. Think how you are in some way like each one of the characters in the story. You have almost half an hour, so there is no need to rush. When something about the story strikes you, reflect on that idea. Be open and allow God's Spirit to lead your thoughts.

> "A man was going down from Jerusalem to Jericho, and fell into the hands of robbers, who stripped him, beat him, and went away, leaving him half dead. Now by chance a priest was going down that road; and when he saw him, he passed by on the other side. So likewise a Levite, when he came to the place and saw him, passed by on the other side. But a Samaritan while traveling came near him; and when he saw him he was moved with pity. He went to him and bandaged his wounds, having poured oil and wine on them. Then he put him on his own animal, brought him to an inn, and took care of him. The next day he took out two denarii, gave them to the innkeeper and said, 'Take care of him; and when I come back, I will repay you whatever more you spend.' "

Another Dimension (15 minutes, set timer)

The purpose of this activity is to look at another dimension of the story. Scripture often presents us with stories that reveal the many facets, or faces, of ourselves.

How am I like the robbers?

I rob not only myself but others as well when I say such things as "Oh, I can't do that," "You're not smart enough," or "I'm too old." Other remarks that indicate there is a robber within us include "It'll never work" and "You wouldn't want to disappoint me, would you?" On the other hand, the robber does not have to *say* anything. A young man who read this story said, "I remember a *look* that I got as a kid, and now I find myself giving others that same look. It says, 'Don't you dare!' I was robbed, and now I rob others." A young woman recalled her inability to accept compliments and how she felt robbed of self-esteem.

How am I like the person beaten on?

Perhaps like Bill, an attorney in his late thirties, we remember times when we wanted to cry for help, but felt beaten down and did not seem to have the energy. Maybe we are like Sandra, a busy forty-five-year-old mother of two, who said, "You get angry when all you want is someone to be compassionate, but no one seems to care about you."

How am I like the priest?

The priest who passes by may be like that part of the self that utters truisms but says them glibly so as not to get involved—truisms such as, "Just pray about it and it will go away," "Be of good cheer," or "Keep a stiff upper lip." We say such things not only to others but to ourselves as well. Remember the last time you put off something by saying, "I'll do it tomorrow"? That is one way of reacting like the priest in the story.

How am I like the Levite?

When we step aside from those who need our help and simply say, "It'll do them good to work it out themselves; they'll learn that way," we are acting like the Levite. We are cool and rational. There are times when that is fine, but such an attitude can be a mask that prevents us from acting with the compassion that is called for and that God expects of us.

How am I like the Samaritan?

The Samaritan has become a romantic and heroic figure whom we often envision as looking for opportunities to dash over without hesitation to do a good deed. Rather than being a do-gooder, the Samaritan might very well have been more like us—wanting to help but feeling hesitant or even fearful. Perhaps the Samaritan asked, "Should I stop, or shouldn't I?" Travelers in those days surely knew of dangers along the road, but the Samaritan chose to stop anyway. Like the Samaritan, we sometimes take the risk and do what we hope others would do for us.

How am I like the innkeeper?

A grandmother who read this story said, "That's me. I'm the innkeeper. In my younger days, I took in stray cats and dogs and frogs and gerbils the kids brought home. As the children grew up, I took in their stray friends and was never sure how many there'd be for breakfast. Now the kids have kids, and I'm back into stray dogs, cats, toys, and grandchildren." A nurse reminded me of another face of the innkeeper. She explained, "I'm the innkeeper who says, 'You pay and I'll provide the room and the care.'" Indeed, there are various ways of being an innkeeper both at home and on the job.

How am I like the beast of burden?

There are days when most of us drag along with bent back and shuffling feet. We do not actually complain, but people looking at us know how burdened we feel. If anyone asked, we might say with a bit of sarcasm, "Oh, I feel fine, but don't worry about me. I'll feel worse tomorrow!"

Shirley is a volunteer church worker who explained why she saw herself so clearly as the beast of burden. "I just let people pile the jobs on me," she admitted. "I'll get them done somehow." Although Shirley would not think of complaining, she would be both happier and more successful if she took on only those jobs she knew she could handle.

Do you ever feel dumped on or overworked? If so, you can identify with the burdened animal.

It is not uncommon for readers of the Samaritan story to say they feel like observers who do not identify with any of the characters, so the final face I mention is that of the onlooker. If reading the story is like watching a movie that does not involve you, or is like looking down at the earth from a cloud, you are reading as an observer. The beautiful thing about God's word is that we can choose to be more than observers by moving purposefully into every Bible story. This requires only that we put aside some of our self-protective attitudes and risk identifying with others. While doing so we may feel some of our own past hurts, but will also understand ourselves more fully. We then have an opportunity to change the way we act toward others as well as toward ourselves.

Break/Rest/Body Movement (15 minutes)

If you are feeling tired and need to rest, set your timer before lying down. If you are going for a walk or doing other gentle body movement, keep track of the time with your watch. The purpose of this activity is to refresh yourself. Have a snack if you like, but whatever you do, continue to reflect in an easy way about the story of the Samaritan and how it helps you see the many facets of your own personality.

Inner Dimension (30 minutes, set timer, get writing materials)

The purpose of this activity is to review what only you and God know about all the faces you wear during a typical week. This review will give you a better understanding of the need to accept yourself as the wonderfully complex person God created. Certainly there are sides of ourselves we do not like, but once we are aware of *all* our faces we can take steps to reveal the very best that is within us.

Write in your notebook or on a separate sheet of paper. Try to think of two to five examples for each of the faces. If you do not complete the activity within thirty minutes, finish it later. If you are done quickly, look more deeply at yourself and add examples you overlooked.

* * *

Example: I'm like the robbers when . . .
1. I tell myself, "You can't do that. It's too hard for you."
2. I tell my daughter, "That's not something girls can do."
3. I tell a co-worker, "I didn't think you'd do it right."
4. I do tasks for others they could and should do themselves.
5. I fail to vote and then speak negatively about those elected.

* * *

These are the faces to think and write about:
I'm like the robbers when I . . . .
I'm like the person beaten on when I . . . .
I'm like the priest when I . . . .
I'm like the Levite when I . . . .
I'm like the Samaritan when I . . . .
I'm like the innkeeper when I . . . .
I'm like the beast of burden when I . . . .

Prayer of Response (10 minutes, set timer)

The purpose of this time is to free you of distractions and allow you to be more attentive to God moving quietly within your mind and heart. Some people like to sit in stillness. Others are drawn to let their body move in prayerful expression. Return to this line (Psalm 139:1) when your attention wanders:
YAHWEH, YOU SEARCH ME AND KNOW ME.

Reflection(10 minutes, set timer, get journaling materials)

Now reflect on what God is revealing to you about your many faces that reveal both weaknesses and strengths. What you write in your notebook or journal must be personal and honest. Among the key ideas you wrote down during the Inner Dimension activity, there is probably one that stands out.

If so, give it more thought. To get an idea of how others have approached this task, consider what a young single woman named Sandra wrote:

> The main insight for me this morning was that I tend to see myself as a beast of burden in my present job. I approach everything as if it is another instance of having something laid on me. I suspect that if I change my own attitude about myself I will be able to say no to some things that I realize I cannot do. This will help me stop feeling so guilty when I don't get things done on time.

Tom, a student, wrote from a different perspective:

> I never permit myself to think of any time when I've been the beaten-on one. The insight I had was that that may be the reason why I get so angry when I hear about anyone out of work or people on welfare. My own inability to see myself as one who needs help hinders me from seeing that anyone would ever need help. Yet, down deep, I truly know I've been beaten on. Maybe that's why my girlfriend says that I'm cold and never seem to need anything. That needs to change.

* * *

Now it is your turn to write.

·What is God helping you to see about yourself today?

·Which of your faces are you aware of in a new way?

·If there is something you would like to change about yourself, outline the steps that would help you change. Make them as practical as possible.

Closing Prayer (Or use the Lord's Prayer or one of the prayers or psalms from Part III)

> O God, I give you thanks for this quiet time of reflection. I know that you love me and call me by name. You know me better than I know myself. May I come to a fuller understanding of who I am and use that knowledge to do your will in the days ahead. I pray in Jesus' name. *Amen.*

S E S S I O N   2

Seeking Forgiveness

And Jesus said, "Neither do I condemn you. Go your way,
and from now on do not sin again."

✳

Create the Environment (5 minutes)

Take a few minutes to create a comfortable environment
for your time alone with God. What you do depends on
whether you are indoors or out, at home or away. If you are
inside, do whatever is necessary to avoid being interrupted by
the telephone or the doorbell. Get comfortable within your
space by turning away from anything distracting and by setting up whatever will help you get into a proper frame of
mind. You may want to open your Bible and place it within
easy reach next to some flowers or a candle.

Will a picture of Jesus, a cross, a crucifix, or an icon help
make you more aware of God's presence? If so, place the item
near the Bible or wherever you can easily look at it without
being distracted. Have at hand everything you may need:
notebook, drawing paper, pens, pencils, art materials.

The objective is to be settled before going further.

Open with Prayer

Almighty God, help me become more attentive. Grant me the
wisdom to see myself clearly. Help me recognize my faults,
and know when to turn to you for forgiveness. Today I seek the
peace that can come only from you. I ask that you forgive me
and help me find the courage I need to forgive myself. *Amen.*

Be Still (10 minutes, set timer)

The purpose of these ten minutes is to relax the body and prepare the mind and heart to become more attentive as you enter into a special time alone with God. Some people do this by sitting quietly, while others find that gentle body movement is helpful. Often when we begin, our minds are cluttered and we feel distracted. Do not fight your thoughts or focus long on those that come to mind. Instead, breathe deeply and evenly as you reflect on scripture. Use this line from scripture (Psalm 55:1) as a touchstone, and come back to it over and over as you remain silent:

HEAR MY PRAYER, O GOD.

Read and Reflect on Scripture (25 minutes, set timer)

The story for this session (John 8:2-11) is that of the woman caught in adultery. Read the story at least three times.

First Reading: Imagine the story from the perspective of Jesus and attempt to sense his feelings and thoughts.

Second Reading: Imagine the story from the perspective of the Pharisees and try to sense their feelings and thoughts.

Third Reading: Imagine the story from the perspective of the woman and try to sense her feelings and thoughts.

You may like to read the story quietly and then again out loud. There is great power in the spoken word, even when it is your voice and you are the audience. You have almost half an hour, so there is no need to rush. When something about the story strikes you, reflect on that idea. Be open to the Word, and allow God to lead your thoughts.

Early in the morning he [Jesus] came again to the temple. All the people came to him and he sat down and began to teach them. The scribes and the Pharisees brought a woman who had been caught in adultery; and making her stand before all of them, they said to him, "Teacher, this woman was caught in the very act of committing adultery. Now in the law Moses commanded us to stone such women. Now what do you

41

say?" They said this to test him, so that they might have some charge to bring against him. Jesus bent down and wrote with his finger on the ground. When they kept on questioning him, he straightened up and said to them, "Let anyone among you who is without sin be the first to throw a stone at her." And once again he bent down and wrote on the ground. When they heard it, they went away, one by one, beginning with the elders; and Jesus was left alone with the woman standing before him. Jesus straightened up and said to her, "Woman, where are they? Has no one condemned you?" She said, "No one, sir." And Jesus said, "Neither do I condemn you. Go your way, and from now on do not sin again."

Another Dimension (15 minutes, set timer)

The purpose of this activity is to look at another dimension of the story. In this case, we will consider four moods that are brought about by what people say or do.

There is a mood of *anticipation* in the crowd that has come to the temple to hear what Jesus will say. The anticipation grows, and we can imagine Jesus speaking.

There is a shift in the mood as the Scribes and Pharisees barge into the midst of the crowd. They have a victim to parade before the group. One can sense a tone of *hostility* as the Pharisees issue a bold and cunning challenge. They attempt to entrap Jesus by pitting him against the Law. In the face of such hostility, what can Jesus possibly do?

Jesus does not deal with the question; he will not be tricked by hostility. Instead, he moves to the level of loving the woman *and* the Pharisees *and* the scribes. Rather than pit himself against the Old Law, he fulfills it with his love. The tone shifts to one of *silent tension* that remains until Jesus says, "Let anyone among you who is without sin be the first to throw a stone at her." It is a most unusual response. In dealing with hypocrisy, Jesus is answering falsehood that masquerades under the guise of keeping the Law. He condemns no one. Instead of arguing against the stoning, Jesus actually gives a suggestion on how it might take place!

At this point in the story, *tension increases.* As Jesus returns to writing on the ground, people slip away one by one until finally only Jesus and the woman remain. She has faced death at the hands of the crowd and now stands before an even more awesome power. Imagine how it feels to be in the presence of someone who faced down such a hostile challenge.

Jesus looks up and asks, "Has no one condemned you?" The woman says, "No one, sir." The dramatic conclusion is brought about by Jesus' simple statement, "Neither do I condemn you. Go your way, and from now on do not sin again."

The tension is gone. Reading this scriptural passage helps us understand that sin is death and that sinning no more is life. Forgiveness separates the two.

This story is about my life and your life, and it raises questions we must face if we are to continue growing as Christians:

•When do I place myself in a position to judge?

•When have I condemned someone else for an action I considered sinful?

•When am I self-righteous in front of others?

•When have I felt God turning to me and saying that I am not condemned, and that I should go and sin no more?

Break/Rest/Body Movement (15 minutes)

If you are feeling tired and need to rest, set your timer before lying down. If you are going for a walk or doing other gentle body movement, keep track of the time with your watch. The purpose of this activity is to refresh yourself. Have a snack if you like, but whatever you do, continue to reflect in an easy way about the story of the woman taken in adultery and your understanding of it.

Inner Dimension (30 minutes, set timer)

This activity focuses on a life review meant to help you discover ways in which you miss the mark and thus fail to live up to your potential.

"Sin" is a word that calls forth a variety of responses. More and more, people are disturbed by their inability to determine what is and what is not sin. What one generation views as sinful, another may consider natural and normal. This is not only distressing to individuals but can actually split congregations into angry camps. One way to get some perspective on how viewpoints can change involves looking back to scripture. The word "sin" in Greek is *hamartia*, which means "missing the mark." Implied in this concept is the fact that there is a recognizable "mark." That mark is the Christian's target.

What is the mark at which the Christian is aiming? What is our call? How we answer depends, at least in part, on our age. For example, a young child quickly learns that we hope to one day be with God, so that becomes the "mark" aimed for. Unfortunately, God may be viewed as a giant police officer who watches over everything and expects absolute obedience. This gives an unfortunate connotation to sin, and the child finds it hard not to confuse God's rules with those of Mom and Dad. Some parents like it that way and use God to achieve good discipline. When this is the case, God's love seems harsh or even nonexistent.

As we grow older and come to understand more about the love of our Creator, we discover that God sent Jesus to be in our midst, to walk with us and touch our lives. We are called to have a living relationship with God. Many new ideas come into focus then. Along with the childhood image and the Ten Commandments, we are confronted with the loving justice revealed through Jesus. What we saw as sin or "missing the mark" must be more broadly defined. Many people prefer the simple right/wrong, black/white, police officer image because it involves clear-cut rules that can be judged rather easily. On the other hand, the addition of Jesus' loving justice often leads to dilemmas that involve making moral decisions without the help of a clearly defined law or rule.

The point I want to make clear is that although people's understanding of sin may differ, every one of us can look within and discover ways we have missed the mark. Yes, we have all sinned and fallen short of the glory of who God called us to be.

* * *

Get out your writing materials.

In the time that remains, do a life review. Write "Missing the Mark" at the top of a sheet of paper. Under that, make a list of ways in which you have not lived up to your potential as a child of God. Begin with the most recent time that you missed the mark, and work back in time. Write down the date, event, or people involved. What you write is for your eyes only, but use abbreviations or fictional names if you would be embarrassed if you lost the list or someone picked it up by mistake.

There is no need to dwell on any of the events; just accept them as facts that are part of your spiritual history. If this exercise is painful, remember the woman in the story. Jesus did not demand that she become something she was not. He accepted her as she was. God does the same with us. Often we wish to hide our past rather than confront it, but remember that there is no time when God does not love us. There is no time—no matter what we have done—when Jesus is not willing to say, "Neither do I condemn you. Go your way, and from now on do not sin again."

Make your *life review* as complete as possible in the remaining time.

Prayer of Response (10 minutes, set timer)

This is a time to take responsibility for your sinfulness, seek forgiveness, and allow God to move quietly within your mind and heart.

Look over the list you made. It reflects a part of you, so acknowledge it, accept it. No matter how foolish or vile you perceive your actions to have been, embrace them now. Then place them at Jesus' feet just as the woman was placed before him. You can do this symbolically by placing your list in your

Bible or on a table or an altar. You may find it meaningful to burn the list as a symbol of accepting that part of yourself and receiving forgiveness.

The purpose of this time is to free you of distractions and allow you to be more attentive to God moving quietly within your mind and heart. Some people like to sit in stillness. Others are drawn to letting their body move in prayerful expression. Whenever your attention wanders, return to this scripture (Psalm 57:1):

HAVE MERCY ON ME, GOD,
HAVE MERCY.

Reflection (10 minutes, set timer, get journaling materials)

Now reflect on how loving and gracious God is to you and to everyone else who turns to God in honesty and truth. Write down or express in another creative way some of your feelings about missing the mark over the years. Is there a way in which you have fallen down again and again? If there is, write about why this has happened. Doing so may help you find the key that will enable you to change.

Close with Prayer (Or use the Lord's Prayer or one of the prayers or psalms from Part III)

O God, after looking at my life, I realize how often I miss the mark. I thank you for your loving gift of forgiveness and ask you to strengthen me. I pray for people everywhere who are mean-spirited and hold grudges. May they come to realize that your love and forgiveness, which Jesus made real in our world, are available to everyone. *Amen.*

Forgiving Others

"And out of pity . . . . forgave him the debt."

✳

Create the Environment (5 minutes)

Take a few minutes to create a comfortable environment for your time alone with God. What you do depends on whether you are indoors or out, at home or away. If you are inside, do whatever is necessary to avoid being interrupted by the telephone or the doorbell. Get comfortable within your space by turning away from anything distracting and by setting up whatever will help you get into a proper frame of mind. You may want to open your Bible and place it within easy reach next to some flowers or a candle.

Will a picture of Jesus, a cross, a crucifix, or an icon help make you more aware of Gods presence? If so, place the item near the Bible or wherever you can easily look at it without being distracted. Have at hand everything you may need: notebook, drawing paper, pens, pencils, art materials.

The objective is to be settled before going further.

Open with Prayer

O God, I know that you have forgiven me many times over. Help me to sense your presence today so that I am encouraged and have the desire to forgive those people whom I feel have offended me. Let me be loving toward them as you have taught me to be, and let me know that I will be forgiven just as I forgive. I pray in Jesus' name. *Amen.*

Be Still (10 minutes, set timer)

The purpose of these ten minutes is to relax the body and prepare the mind and heart to become more attentive as you enter into a special time alone with God. Some people do this by sitting quietly, while others find that gentle body movement is helpful. Often when we begin, our minds are cluttered and we feel distracted. Do not fight your thoughts or focus long on those that come to mind. Instead, breathe deeply and evenly as you reflect on scripture. Use a short prayer of your own or this scripture (Psalm 42:2) as a touchstone, and come back to it over and over as you remain silent:

MY SOUL THIRSTS FOR GOD.

Read and Reflect on Scripture (25 minutes, set timer)

The story for this session (Matthew 18:23-35) is that of the settlement of accounts. Read the story over and over. You may like to read it quietly and then again out loud. There is great power in the spoken word, even when the voice is your own and you are the audience. Consider how the story applies to times when you have been in a position to be forgiving. Be open and allow God to lead your thoughts.

"For this reason the kingdom of heaven may be compared to a king who wished to settle accounts with his slaves. When he began the reckoning, one who owed him ten thousand talents was brought to him; and, as he couldn't pay, his lord ordered him to be sold, together with his wife and children and all his possessions, and payment to be made. So the slave fell on his knees before him, saying, 'Have patience with me, and I will pay you everything.' And out of pity for him the lord of that slave released him and forgave him the debt. But that same slave, as he went out, came upon one of his fellow slaves who owed him a hundred denarii; and seizing him by the throat, he said, 'Pay what you owe.' Then his fellow slave fell down and pleaded with him, 'Have patience with me, and I will pay you.' But he refused; then he went and threw him into prison until he would pay the debt. When his fellow slaves saw what had happened, they were greatly distressed, and they went and reported to their lord all that had taken place. Then his lord summoned him and said to him, 'You wicked slave! I forgave you all that debt because you pleaded with me. Should you not have had mercy on your fellow slave, as I had mercy on you?' And in anger his lord handed him over to be tortured until he would pay his entire debt. So my heavenly Father will also do to every one of you, if you do not forgive your brother or sister from your heart."

Another Dimension (15 minutes, set timer)

This time is an opportunity to look at another dimension of the story. In this case, we see an example of what happens when a person has sight but no vision insofar as forgiveness is concerned. Anyone who has fallen behind on paying bills can certainly identify with the panic the slave feels when the king calls for an immediate settling of accounts. The slave, his wife and children, and their possessions are to be sold so that the debt can be repaid. There is no time to think, no time to borrow. The day of reckoning is at hand. In desperation the slave falls to his knees and requests an extension of time, just as we would do if the bank called to foreclose on our car or home or farm or business.

The slave's desperate plea brings forth the kind of compassionate response that was as unusual in biblical times as in our own day. Occasionally (usually during the Christmas season) we read a newspaper story about someone forgiving or paying off the debt of another, but such events are so extraordinary that they make the news.

We can imagine how the slave feels upon hearing the king's response to his plea. His debt is forgiven and the weight of ruin has been lifted from his shoulders. He rises from his knees and goes his way. The sad story appears to have a happy ending and reminds us of an old-time melodrama in which the heroine tied to the railroad tracks is saved from disaster at the last second. But in this case the story is not yet over. As the slave goes about his business, he appears to have learned nothing from his experience. All he can see are his own selfish interests. He has sight, but no vision. Self-interest overshadows him, and he refuses to do to others the kindness that has been done to him. When it comes to being forgiving, he has a very short memory.

What about us? Do we see the right thing being done and pass along the kindness, or do we, like the slave, have sight but no vision? Think for a moment of all the times we have prayed the phrase "Forgive us our trespasses as we forgive those who trespass against us." We pray the words, but do we really mean them? *Do we truly want God to forgive us just as we forgive others? Do we forgive others as we have been forgiven?*

Mike was in jail serving time for a felony when he first heard Jesus' response to Peter's question about how many times he must forgive another's sins. "I was struck that Jesus seemed to say so clearly to me that I've been forgiven more than I can ever forgive someone else," Mike said. "For a long time I didn't think I could ever be forgiven by God. But one day it connected. I made a list right then and there and started forgiving people."

Not all of us are quite so forthright. Sandra, who came to me for spiritual direction, said, "When I owe something to someone I generally send it by mail. There's something about not wanting to see the person face to face when I'm in their debt. And then, I usually don't even like sending a letter with the payment. I try to make it as impersonal as possible. And I've noticed that the person to whom I'm in debt never mentions it either."

Truly, the slave in the story who is forgiven and then does not forgive his friend is a universal character with whom we can all identify in some way.

·When it comes to forgiveness, are you shortsighted? Or do you have a clear vision of the need to both seek and grant forgiveness?

•Have you ever been in Mike's position and realized that the story Jesus told applies directly to you and your life?

•Are you at all like Sandra, who tries to avoid those to whom she is in debt?

Break/Rest/Body Movement (15 minutes)

If you are feeling tired and need to rest, set your timer before lying down. If you are going for a walk or doing other gentle body movement, keep track of the time with your watch. Refresh yourself. Have a snack if you like, but whatever you do, continue to reflect in an easy way about your attitude toward forgiving others.

Inner Dimension (30 minutes, set timer, get writing materials)

The purpose of this activity is to review your life in a systematic way in order to recognize hurtful relationships that are still in need of healing—healing that can best come about through forgiveness on your part.

1. At the top of a sheet of paper, write: "People who have hurt me, harmed me, or done something against me."

2. Pray the Lord's Prayer.

3. Spend fifteen minutes making a list of people who have hurt, harmed, or done something against you. Begin in the present and work back in time. There is no need to go over the events in detail; just write down a name or initials.

4. At the end of the time, reset the timer for another fifteen minutes and pray the Lord's Prayer again.

5. Spend the remainder of your time forgiving the people on your list, one by one. Imagine that the person is with you, and simply say, "_(name)_ I forgive you." Then, in your own words, pray for that person in a prayer such as this:

God, you have forgiven me and love me as I am. Release any hurt or anger I have toward __(name)__ and bless our relationship. I seek only good for __(name)__ . Transform our hearts so that we can forgive one another. *Amen.*

6. Continue down your list. There may be some people you are not ready to forgive. That is all right. You can come back to this session another time and repeat it. Do what you can now. Trust in God. Even if you are able to forgive only one person in the allotted time, you have begun to live out the prayer that Jesus taught us to pray.

Prayer of Response (10 minutes, set timer)

The purpose of this time is to free you of distractions and allow you to be more attentive to God moving quietly within your mind and heart. Some people like to sit in stillness. Others are drawn to let their body move in prayerful expression. Whenever your attention wanders, return to this scripture (Psalm 66:19):

TRULY GOD HAS LISTENED.

Reflection (10 minutes, set timer, get writing materials)

Now reflect on what God is revealing to you about forgiveness. What you write in your notebook or journal should reveal your deepest response. If you feel tearful, allow yourself to cry. For an idea of how others have approached this task, consider the following journal entry by Joan, a widow in her sixties:

> After making my list of people who had done something against me, I was aware that I was relieved to have it out on paper. Even though some names were painful to remember, and I had forgiven them long ago, I discovered there was still hurt or some anger there.
>
> So I asked the Lord to release me from all that was holding me back. I found it interesting that some of the people had died already, and yet when I asked their forgiveness it was like they were right in front of me.
>
> I didn't make it through my list today, but I didn't feel like I had to either. I know that I've gotten names out into the open, and now I can be freer than ever before.

Now it is your turn to write.

·Was forgiving difficult?

·How did your feelings change as you went on?

·What prevented you from forgiving before?

Consider sending a note or letter to anyone from whom you have been cut off but now feel able to recontact in a spirit of love.

Close with Prayer (Or use the Lord's Prayer or one of the prayers or psalms from Part III)

O God, sometimes I forget I am under your protection and that you love me beyond what I can imagine. Thank you for forgiving all my trespasses. Help me to go on being released from all hurt and anger toward others and to be ever mindful that it is up to me to be forgiving. I ask this in Jesus' name. *Amen.*

Receiving New Sight

[Jesus] asked him, "What do you want me to do for you?"

✳

Create the Environment (5 minutes)

Take a few minutes to create a comfortable environment for your time alone. What you do depends on whether you are indoors or out, at home or away. If you are inside, do whatever is necessary to avoid being interrupted by the telephone or doorbell. Get comfortable in the space by turning away from anything distracting and setting up whatever will help you get into a proper frame of mind. You may want to open your Bible within easy reach next to a candle or flowers.

Will a picture of Jesus, a cross, a crucifix, or an icon help make you more aware of God's presence? If so, place the item near the Bible or wherever you can easily look at it without being distracted. Have at hand everything you may need: notebook, drawing paper, pens, pencils, art materials. The objective is to be settled before going further.

Open with Prayer

O God, I humbly place myself in your presence. At times it is difficult for me to realize I am created in your image and likeness, because I know there are parts of my life that need to be healed. Help me today to be open to the love that Jesus makes real. Help me to see every day in a new light and make the best use of the time you have granted me. I pray in Jesus' name. *Amen.*

Receiving New Sight

Be Still (10 minutes, set timer)

The purpose of these ten minutes is to relax the body and prepare the mind and heart to become more attentive as you enter into a special time alone with God. Some people do so by sitting quietly; others find gentle body movement is helpful. Often when we begin, our minds are cluttered and we feel distracted. Do not fight your thoughts or focus long on those that come to mind. Instead, breathe deeply and evenly as you reflect on scripture. Use this scripture (Psalm 61:1) as a touchstone, coming back to it over and over as you remain silent:

HEAR MY CRY, O GOD; LISTEN TO MY PRAYER.

Read and Reflect on Scripture (25 minutes, set timer)

The story for this session (Luke 18:35-43) is that of the blind man who was made to see. Read the story over and over. You may like to read it quietly and then again out loud. There is great power in the spoken word, even when it is your voice and you are the audience. Try to enter the story by imagining yourself at the city gate where beggars and merchants clamor for attention as people move along the road. You have almost half an hour, so there is no need to rush. When something in the story strikes you, reflect on that idea. Be open to the Word, allowing God's Spirit to lead your thoughts.

As he [Jesus] approached Jericho, a blind man was sitting by the roadside begging. When he heard a crowd going by, he asked what was happening. They told him, "Jesus of Nazareth is passing by." Then he shouted, "Jesus, Son of David, have mercy on me!" Those who were in front sternly ordered him to be quiet; but he shouted even more loudly, "Son of David, have mercy on me!" Jesus stood still and ordered the man to be brought to him; and when he came near, he asked him, "What do you want me to do for you?" He said, "Lord, let me see again." Jesus said to him, "Receive your sight; your faith has saved you." Immediately he regained his sight and followed him, glorifying God; and all the people, when they saw it, praised God.

Another Dimension (15 minutes, set timer)

The purpose of this activity is to look at another dimension of the story and the special meaning it can have for us.

Even those of us who can see sometimes find ourselves "in the dark" about some aspect of our life. Whenever we are in need of healing but are unsure how to proceed, the story of the blind man gives us direction. Jesus did not seek out the blind man. Rather, the blind man sought out Jesus, and that is exactly what we must do. But there is more. Jesus asks that we speak for ourselves and be specific concerning our need. Jesus asks the blind man, "What do you want me to do for you?" The man responds, "Lord, let me see again."

These two important points—personally seeking out Jesus and telling him our specific needs—are the keys to receiving new sight. Nowhere in any of the miracles of Jesus does the person who yearns for help respond, "Just do anything you'd like to do, Jesus." The requests are always specific, reminding us that we must take responsibility for our need and ask for the healing change. Do you generally seek out God? Can you be specific in your requests, or do you consider that selfish?

Often one of our difficulties is the inability to define exactly what is troubling us. When we are not well physically, we can check into the hospital while other people test us until they find out what is wrong. It is not quite the same when we are unwell spiritually. Even if we find someone who can help guide us, we still must do the work ourselves. The first step is believing—believing as the blind man did that Jesus has the power to heal whatever is causing us dis-ease.

Break/Rest/Body Movement (15 minutes)

If you are feeling tired and need to rest, set your timer before lying down. If you are going to walk or do other gentle body movement, keep track of the time with your watch. This is a moment to refresh yourself. Have a snack if you like, but whatever you do, continue to reflect in an easy way about the story of the blind man and your understanding of it.

Inner Dimension (20 minutes, set timer, get writing materials)

The purpose of this activity is to unveil something you are currently in the "dark" about, but which is going to need healing somewhere along the spiritual path you are following. Print the word "CRISES" at the top of a sheet of paper. Then list all the large and small "crisis situations" that are, and have been, a part of your life. What is a crisis? It may be a deadline missed at school or the office, a forgotten appointment, a missed birthday, or a guilty feeling about a personal relationship. It does not have to be a life-or-death situation, but it should be an event that makes your life run less smoothly than you like. Begin with the most recent crisis and the approximate date it occurred: today, a few days ago, last week, last month, at Christmas. Then work back in time.

* * *

Example:

Yesterday.
Disagreement with boss who never seems to listen to me.
Late for dinner.
Had a flat.

Last Friday.
Lost temper, got mad at kids at breakfast, swore at them.
Missed an important sale. Customer didn't seem to like me.

A week ago Friday.
Felt frustrated all day.
Drank too much before going home. Know it had something to do with the way I'm feeling at work.

* * *

Don't worry about remembering exact times and dates. As you work back, ask yourself, "When was the time before that?" and make notes about crisis events that come to mind.

Inner Dimension (10 minutes, set timer)

Now look through your crisis list and see if you can discover a pattern. This is the entry a forty-year-old husband

and father made in his journal after seeking patterns in his crisis list:

> The task wasn't as hard as I thought it would be. I didn't think I'd be able to recall many situations, but God just seemed to be leading me to remember. One crisis memory triggered another. I was able to remember some things from childhood that I hadn't remembered in years. And I was amazed to see that a pattern was very clear to me. Many of the crisis situations I listed were times when I was feeling like I had to prove myself. This is what I can bring before God— my need to prove myself.

Beverly, a nurse who was single again after a divorce, had quite a different experience when she did this activity.

> After doing all this, some of which was painful, I became aware that I didn't *see* a pattern as much as *feel* one. I had the feeling of being a victim in situations and powerless to do anything. I immediately thought of one of my patients in intensive care who had told me he felt powerless and how at the time I had felt a strange identification with him. I know I'll be different when I see him again.

Look for a pattern in the entries on your crisis list. Perhaps it is similar to patterns that others have identified.
·Do I always have to have my own way?
·Is fear of failure holding me back?
·Am I forever waiting for something to happen?
·Do I look to others to save me and feel disappointed when no one does?
·Do I create problems to get attention?
As clearly as possible, clarify and write down your way of acting or feeling. Once you recognize your old way of responding, you are not in the dark about it and can turn it over to God.

Prayer of Response (10 minutes, set timer)

The purpose of this activity is to realize that Jesus is waiting for us to tell him what we want. Look at the pattern you discovered. The pattern may have been:

·something you were not aware of,

·something you chose not to recognize about yourself,

·something you recognized but haven't dealt with openly,

·something you may have been working on and now believe you can take a step further or even finish.

Like the blind man in the story, you were still in the dark. But now, while sitting quietly or doing gentle body movement, you can admit your need to Jesus and receive new insights. Enter into a prayer dialogue with Jesus, speaking with him even more intimately than you would with any other friend. Come back to this thought again and again:

Jesus asks, "What do you want me to do for you?"

You answer, "God, I want (tell God what you want done)."

Reflection (10 minutes, set timer, get writing materials)

Now reflect on what you have discovered, and commit yourself to some new behavior patterns. It is important that you come out of the darkness willingly, remembering and believing that Jesus strengthens you when you do. Be as objective about yourself as possible. Should I be . . .

·paying more attention to others?

·taking better care of my health?

·praying or reading more?

·working on a personal relationship?

Close with Prayer (The Lord's Prayer or a prayer from Part III)

God, I know there are times when I am in the dark about the way I act toward myself and others. Like the blind man, I, too, call out for help. Although my faith is weak, I believe you hear all prayers. Today, I pray especially that_____. Please help me to see anew and to be a light to others. *Amen.*

Calling to Jesus

Peter answered him, "Lord, if it is you, command me
to come to you on the water."

✳

Create the Environment (5 minutes)

Take a few minutes to create a comfortable environment
for your time alone with God. What you do depends on
whether you are indoors or out, at home or away. If you are
inside, do whatever is necessary to avoid being interrupted by
the telephone or the doorbell. Get comfortable within your
space by turning away from anything distracting and by setting up whatever will help you get into a proper frame of
mind. You may want to open your Bible and place it within
easy reach next to some flowers or a candle.

Will a picture of Jesus, a cross, a crucifix, or an icon help
make you more aware of God's presence? If so, place the item
near the Bible or wherever you can easily look at it without
being distracted. Have at hand everything you may need:
notebook, drawing paper, pens, pencils, art materials.

The objective is to be settled before going further.

Open with Prayer

Almighty God, I feel a need that only you can answer. I do not
like to give up control, and at times I try to go it alone. Give me the
patience to be more attentive to your presence in my life. Help me to
trust enough to admit my needs and to give my power over to you.
Then guide me to listen for your response. *Amen.*

Be Still (10 minutes, set timer)

The purpose of these ten minutes is to relax the body and prepare the mind and heart to become more attentive as you enter into a special time alone with God. Some people do this by sitting quietly, while others find that gentle body movement is helpful. Often when we begin, our minds are cluttered and we feel distracted. Do not fight your thoughts or focus long on those that come to mind. Instead, breathe deeply and evenly as you reflect on scripture. Use this scripture (Psalm 54:1) as a touchstone, and come back to it over and over as you remain silent:

SAVE ME, O GOD, BY THE POWER OF YOUR NAME.

Read and Reflect on Scripture (25 minutes, set timer)

The story for this session (Matthew 14:22-33) is that of Jesus walking on the water. Read the story over and over. You may like to read it quietly and then again out loud. There is great power in the spoken word, even when it is your voice and you are the audience. Think how you are in some way like the characters in the story. You have nearly half an hour, so there is no need to rush. When something about the story strikes you, reflect on that idea. Be open to the Word, and allow God to lead your thoughts.

> Immediately he [Jesus] made the disciples get into the boat and go on ahead to the other side, while he dismissed the crowds. And after he had dismissed the crowds, he went up the mountain by himself to pray. When evening came, he was there alone, but by this time the boat, battered by the waves, was far from the land, for the wind was against them. And early in the morning he came walking toward them on the sea. But when the disciples saw him walking on the sea, they were terrified, saying, "It is a ghost!" And they cried out in fear. But immediately Jesus spoke to them and said, "Take heart, it is I; do not be afraid."
>
> Peter answered him, "Lord, if it is you, command me to come to you on the water." He said, "Come." So Peter got out

of the boat, started walking on the water, and came toward Jesus. But when he noticed the strong wind, he became frightened, and beginning to sink, he cried out, "Lord, save me!" Jesus immediately reached out his hand and caught him, saying to him, "You of little faith, why did you doubt?" When they got into the boat, the wind ceased. And those in the boat worshipped him, saying, "Truly you are the Son of God."

Another Dimension (15 minutes, set timer)

The purpose of this activity is to look at another dimension of the story and the special meaning it can have for us. In this story, we will examine three ideas in detail.

First, consider the placement of this story in the Christian Testament. It follows immediately after the feeding of 5,000 people with five loaves and two fish. The disciples are in the midst of this crowd and observe firsthand that after people have eaten their fill, there are plenty of leftovers. Within a few hours, however, the disciples face a problem that does not seem any more demanding than the feeding of the hungry, yet they appear to have forgotten Jesus' care and concern. Sometimes we too quickly forget past blessings.

A second dimension to consider about this story is the role of the wind. Although storms come up quickly on the Lake of Gennesaret, it is the wind's possible *direction* and not its stormy force that we will consider. The boat is heading into the wind. Jesus, walking toward the boat, is walking into the wind. When Peter gets out of the boat to go toward Jesus, he has the wind at his back.

Think about the difference between a head wind and a tail wind. We have all struggled against a head wind and understand what effort it takes to walk into one. But think about the wind that comes from behind, the wind that might be pushing Peter faster than he wanted to go. Perhaps Peter felt himself losing control over the situation and was not quite ready. We can be that way ourselves, pushed so rapidly by the Spirit toward God's wondrous love that we are not quite prepared.

The third dimension to ponder is the call to have faith and move beyond whatever appears to be a secure position; to believe that there is power we have not yet experienced. Certainly the boat in the story does not seem to be a very comfortable refuge in a storm. It does, however, remind us that nothing earthly offers the security that Jesus offers. And yet a rocking boat is sometimes better than nothing!

Break/Rest/Body Movement (15 minutes)
If you are feeling tired and need to rest, set your timer before lying down. If you are going to walk or do other gentle body movement, keep track of the time with your watch. Refresh yourself. Have a snack if you like, but whatever you do, continue to reflect in an easy way about the story of Peter and Jesus meeting on the water.

Inner Dimension (30 minutes, set timer, get writing materials)
The purpose of this activity is to look within your own life and see how God is calling you. What security is God asking you to step away from in faith in order to experience a new blessing? Divide your paper into three sections, and give the sections these headings:

1	2	3
My blessings	My boat	Times I've felt the Spirit moving me faster toward Jesus than I would like to go

* * *

Under each of these headings, make specific notes that describe your spiritual journey thus far in life.
Column 1: In what physical, mental, spiritual, and emotional ways do I feel God has gifted me?
Column 2: What gives me a sense of security and would be difficult to let go of?

Column 3: When have I felt the Spirit moving me faster than I would like to go toward Jesus? In this column, reflect on those times when you felt that God was dealing with you a little too fast. Some people find this the most difficult question, so consider such things as prayer experiences, the death of a loved one and your response to it, the call of an evangelist, your reaction to an inspiring book or movie, a news story about someone's need. Think of a time when you said, "Yes, God, but not right now, please."

Prayer of Response (10 minutes, set timer)

The purpose of this activity is to become more attentive to thanking God for your blessings. Look over your list of blessings. Although these have been a part of your life, what has already happened to you is only a taste of what is to come.

Sit still and return to this scripture (Psalm 57:7) whenever your attention wanders:

MY HEART IS STEADFAST, GOD.

Reflection (10 minutes, set timer, get journaling materials)

Now reflect on the reading and what it reveals about your spiritual life. This is what Jerry, a young computer programmer, wrote in his journal:

> I find that I can really identify with Peter calling to Jesus, and so I thought of the times that I've called out to Jesus to have me come to him. Then I was aware that I've always had problems stepping out of the boat. So I decided that maybe this scripture was calling me to look at what I really consider security for myself and what I refuse to get out of or let go of.

An elderly woman named Ruth wrote this reflection:

> I was struck by the fact that the disciples had just seen a miracle of feeding more than 5,000 people and yet how easily they were distracted from what they had just experienced and got caught up in a new problem. That is so much like my life,

it seems. If I really hear myself talk when i say, "Oh, I wish the Lord would be active in my life," I'd remember the many times the Lord has simply overwhelmed me with goodness. Maybe I don't rejoice in those events enough.

Pat, an English teacher, responded to the reading by sketching a simple drawing of two clasped hands, Jesus' hand coming out of sunshine, and hers) coming out of darkness and chaotic storm clouds.

·What is Jesus calling you to right now?
·From what security is God asking you to step away from in faith to experience a new blessing?

Close with Prayer (Or use the Lord's Prayer or one of the prayers or psalms from Part III)
O God, you have called me time and time again to come toward you. Often I have refused to step away from my security. For these times, I am sorry and seek forgiveness. At other times, I have stepped forward in faith and realized many blessings. For this I now give thanks. Let me feel the presence of your love and not be afraid of moving into a deep and everlasting faith. Continue to fill me with your powerful Spirit. *Amen.*

S E S S I O N 6

Freedom
Jesus said to them, "Unbind him, and let him go."

✳

Create the Environment (5 minutes)

Take a few minutes to create a comfortable environment for your time alone with God. What you do depends on whether you are indoors or out, at home or away. If you are inside, do whatever is necessary to avoid being interrupted by the telephone or the doorbell. Get comfortable within your space by turning away from anything distracting and by setting up whatever will help you get into a proper frame of mind. You may want to open your Bible and place it within easy reach next to some flowers or a candle.

Will a picture of Jesus, a cross, a crucifix, or an icon help make you more aware of God's presence? If so, place the item near the Bible or wherever you can easily look at it without being distracted. Have at hand everything you may need: notebook, drawing paper, pens, pencils, art materials.

The objective is to be settled before going further.

Open with Prayer

God, source of freeing love, I give you thanks for all the wonders you place before me. At times I become self-centered and bound up by my own small world. In seeing my needs so clearly, I forget the needs of others. Today, as I place myself in your presence, help me to understand and accept the freeing power of love that Jesus offers. *Amen.*

Be Still (10 minutes, set timer)

The purpose of these ten minutes is to relax the body and prepare the mind and heart to become more attentive as you enter into a special time alone with God. Some people do this by sitting quietly, while others find that gentle body movement is helpful. Often when we begin, our minds are cluttered and we feel distracted. Do not fight your thoughts or focus long on those that come to mind. Instead, breathe deeply and evenly as you reflect on scripture. Use this scripture (Psalm 29:4) as a touchstone, and come back to it over and over as you remain silent:

THE VOICE OF GOD IS POWERFUL;
THE VOICE OF YAHWEH IS FULL OF MAJESTY.

Read and Reflect on Scripture (25 minutes, set timer)

The story for this session (John 11:1-44) is that of Lazarus being raised from the dead. Read the story at least twice. You may like to read it silently the first time and then out loud. There is great power in the spoken word, even when it is your voice and you are the audience. You have almost half an hour, so there is no need to rush. When something about the story strikes you, reflect on that idea. Be open to the Word, and allow God to lead your thoughts.

Now a certain man was ill, Lazarus of Bethany, the village of Mary and her sister Martha. Mary was the one who anointed the Lord with perfume and wiped his feet with her hair; her brother Lazarus was ill. So the sisters sent a message to Jesus, "Lord, he whom you love is ill." But when Jesus heard it, he said, "This illness does not lead to death; rather it is for God's glory, so that the Son of God may be glorified through it." Accordingly, though Jesus loved Martha and her sister and Lazarus, after having heard that Lazarus was ill, he stayed two days longer in the place where he was.

Then after this he said to the disciples, "Let us go to Judea again." The disciples said to him, "Rabbi, the Jews were just now trying to stone you, and are you going there again?"

Jesus answered, "Are there not twelve hours of daylight? Those who walk during the day do not stumble, because they see the light of this world. But those who walk at night stumble, because the light is not in them." After saying this, he told them, "Our friend Lazarus has fallen asleep, but I am going there to awaken him." The disciples said to him, "Lord, if he has fallen asleep, he will be all right." Jesus, however, had been speaking about his death, but they thought that he was referring merely to sleep. Then Jesus told them plainly, "Lazarus is dead. For your sake I am glad I was not there, so that you may believe. But let us go to him." Thomas, who was called the Twin, said to his fellow disciples, "Let us also go, that we may die with him."

When Jesus arrived, he found that Lazarus had already been in the tomb four days. Now Bethany was near Jerusalem, some two miles away, and many of the Jews had come to Martha and Mary to console them about their brother. When Martha heard that Jesus was coming, she went and met him, while Mary stayed at home. Martha said to Jesus, "Lord, if you had been here, my brother would not have died. But even now I know that God will give you whatever you ask of him." Jesus said to her, "Your brother will rise again." Martha said to him, "I know that he will rise again in the resurrection on the last day." Jesus said to her, "I am the resurrection and the life. Those who believe in me, even though they die, will live, and everyone who lives and believes in me will never die. Do you believe this?" She said to him, "Yes, Lord, I believe that you are the Messiah, the Son of God, the one coming into the world."

When she had said this, she went back and called her sister Mary, and told her privately, "The Teacher is here and is calling for you." And when she heard it, she got up quickly and went to him. Now Jesus had not yet come to the village, but was still at the place where Martha had met him. The Jews who were with her in the house, consoling her, saw Mary get up quickly and go out. They followed her because they thought that she was going to the tomb to weep there. When Mary came where Jesus was and saw him, she knelt at his feet and said to him, "Lord, if you had been here, my brother would not have died." When Jesus saw her weeping, and the Jews who came with her also weeping, he was greatly disturbed in spirit and deeply moved. He said, "Where have you laid him?" They said to him, "Lord, come and see." Jesus began to weep. So the Jews said, "See how he loved him!" But some of them said, "Could not he who opened the eyes of the blind man have kept this man from dying?"

Then Jesus, again greatly disturbed, came to the tomb. It was a cave, and a stone was lying against it. Jesus said, "Take away the stone." Martha, the sister of the dead man, said to him, "Lord, already there is a stench because he has been dead four days." Jesus said to her, "Did I not tell you that if you believed, you would see the glory of God?" So they took away the stone. And Jesus looked upward and said, "Father, I thank you for having heard me. I knew that you always hear me, but I have said this for the sake of the crowd standing here, so that they may believe that you sent me." When he had said this, he cried with a loud voice, "Lazarus, come out!" The dead man came out, his hands and feet bound with strips of cloth, and his face wrapped in a cloth. Jesus said to them, "Unbind him, and let him go."

Another Dimension (15 minutes, set timer)

Now let us look at another dimension of the story to discover personal meanings it may have for us.

One way to study this story is to think of it as a play with six scenes. The scenes have characters and actions with which we may identify or from which we may gain insights for spiritual growth.

Scene 1: Jesus and his disciples receive the message about Lazarus, and there is misunderstanding. Jesus has an understanding and a plan that the others do not share. They are confused, but already we see Jesus taking the action forward. There is even a touch of humor in this scene as Jesus' words fly over the heads of his followers. The disciples do not see what Jesus is getting at when he talks about walking in the daylight because people can see the light of the world.

Scene 2: Jesus and his friends arrive at Bethany, where many Jews have come from Jerusalem to share in the grieving. Someone tells Martha that Jesus has arrived, and we have a dialogue between Martha and Jesus that is theological in tone.

Scene 3: Martha returns to the house where Mary and the other women are grieving. Perhaps they are sitting and talking softly as we might be in a funeral home or at the home of the deceased. Martha whispers to Mary, who then bolts out of the house. Mary goes to Jesus and blurts out what is on her mind. The tone of the conversation is quite different. Where Martha's theological talk might be symbolic of the rational aspect of ourselves, Mary's words might be the intuitive or emotive aspect. Notice, though, that now both women are present with Jesus as the movement of the drama continues.

Scene 4: This is a short but pivotal scene where Jesus stands at center stage. Jesus weeps and then says, "Where have you laid him?" and "Take away the stone." Martha's blunt words emphasize what she sees as the awful reality: "already there is a stench."

Scene 5: There is a dramatic moving of the stone. The end is swiftly approaching, and Jesus places himself in the power of the Father and in the midst of the people. He makes it clear what he is about.

Scene 6: Even Jesus is in the shadows as the last scene opens with everyone looking to the tomb. One can feel the tension as Jesus calls, "Lazarus, come out!" Into the blazing light comes the man Lazarus, wrapped and bound. After that dramatic moment, Jesus concludes with the final, freeing words: "Unbind him, and let him go."

Break/Rest/Body Movement (10 minutes)

If you are feeling tired and need to rest, set your timer before lying down. If you are going to walk or do other gentle body movement, keep track of the time with your watch. The purpose of this activity is to refresh yourself. Have a snack if you like, but continue to reflect on the story of Lazarus.

Inner Dimension (30 minutes, set timer)

Now you have the opportunity to discover how some or all of the Lazarus story relates to your journey with God.

At some time in life, each of us experiences the essence of the scenes outlined in the dramatization of the story. Recall, if you can, a time of misunderstanding and confusion when you were unable to see what plan God intended for you. This was probably a time when you did not understand the signs and had to plod along in trusting.

Now think of another instance when you were confronted by words or actions that you felt were from God, or someone else you trusted, and tried to figure it out. Maybe you got into theological talk, the way Martha did. There is nothing wrong with this approach, but be aware that this analytical approach might ignore the "heart" of the question.

Has there ever been a time when, like Mary, you rushed to Jesus with your hurt and realized he not only knew what you were feeling but shared your pain?

Think back to an event that you kept buried like Lazarus behind the stone and were not sure you wanted revealed. Did you eventually "take away the stone" and confront the issue, or are you still keeping it buried?

There was a time when you sensed Jesus moving closer and closer to you. How did you respond?

Recall, if you can, a time when you felt the power of God close at hand, had a deep sense of expectation, and then enjoyed a wondrous sense of release.

Each of us is Lazarus, and as we recall the details of the story, we can realize anew that we have been set free by the powerful words of Jesus.

Prayer of Response (10 minutes, set timer)

The purpose of this time is to free you of distractions and allow you to be more attentive to God moving quietly within your mind and heart. Some people like to sit in stillness. Others are drawn to let their body move in prayerful expression.

Whenever your attention wanders, return to this scripture (Psalm 51:10):
CREATE A PURE HEART IN ME, O MY GOD.

Reflection (10 minutes, set timer, get writing materials)
As you write or draw, recognize that God calls you forth to freedom. Make a note or sketch of some personal insight or rediscovery that has come from your work with the story of Lazarus.

Close with Prayer (Or use the Lord's Prayer or one of the prayers or psalms from Part III)
God, our Creator, I thank you for sending Jesus to be the light of the world. Help me see that I am free from sin and darkness. Like Lazarus, I hear a call to come into the light. Encourage me to answer your call, and continue to fill me with love so that I might be a light in the lives of people I know. I ask this in Jesus' name. *Amen.*

Sharing God's Word

"My soul magnifies the Lord."

✳

Create the Environment (5 minutes)

Take a few minutes to create a comfortable environment for your time alone with God. What you do depends on whether you are indoors or out, at home or away. If you are inside, do whatever is necessary to avoid being interrupted by the telephone or the doorbell. Get comfortable within your space by turning away from anything distracting and by setting up whatever will help you get into a proper frame of mind. You may want to open your Bible and place it within easy reach next to some flowers or a candle.

Will a picture of Jesus, a cross, a crucifix, or an icon help make you more aware of Gods presence? If so, place the item near the Bible or wherever you can easily look at it without being distracted. Have everything you may need at hand: notebook, drawing paper, pens, pencils, art materials.

The objective is to be settled before going further.

Open with Prayer

O God, you have called to me in the depths of my mind and heart. Through the people in my life, you have provided support and love. Continue to fill me with your Spirit that I may remember and give thanks for those who have helped me grow. Bless these relationships as I take this time in prayer and reflection. *Amen.*

Be Still (10 minutes, set timer)

The purpose of these ten minutes is to relax the body and prepare the mind and heart to become more attentive as you enter into a special time alone with God. Some people do this by sitting quietly, while others find that gentle body movement is helpful. Often when we begin, our minds are cluttered and we feel distracted. Do not fight your thoughts or focus long on those that come to mind. Instead, breathe deeply and evenly as you reflect on scripture. Use a short prayer or this scripture (Psalm 92:1) as a touchstone, and come back to it over and over as you remain silent:

O YAHWEH, IT IS GOOD TO GIVE YOU THANKS.

Read and Reflect on Scripture (25 minutes, set timer)

The story for this session (Luke 1:39-55) is that of the visitation of Mary to her cousin. Read the story over and over. You may like to read it quietly and then again out loud. There is great power in the spoken word, even when it is your voice and you are the audience. Think how the story applies to your life at this time. You have almost half an hour, so there is no need to rush. When something about the story strikes you, reflect on that idea. Be open to the Word, and allow God's Spirit to lead your thoughts.

> In those days Mary set out and went with haste to a Judean town in the hill country, where she entered the house of Zechariah and greeted Elizabeth. When Elizabeth heard Mary's greeting, the child leaped in her womb. And Elizabeth was filled with a loud cry. "Blessed are you among women, and blessed is the fruit of your womb. And why has this happened to me, that the mother of my Lord comes to me? For as soon as I heard the sound of your greeting, the child in my womb leaped for joy. And blessed is she who believed that there would be a fulfillment of what was spoken to her by the Lord." And Mary said,
> "My soul magnifies the Lord,
> and my spirit rejoices in God my Savior,

for he has looked with favor on
the lowliness of his servant.
Surely, from now on all
generations will call me blessed;
for the Mighty One has done
great things for me
and holy is his name.
His mercy is for those who fear him
from generation to generation.
He has shown strength with his arm;
he has scattered the proud in
the thoughts of their hearts.
He has brought down the
powerful from their thrones,
and lifted up the lowly;
he has filled the hungry with good things,
and sent the rich away empty.
He has helped his servant Israel,
in remembrance of his mercy,
according to the promise he made to our ancestors,
to Abraham and to his descendants forever."

Another Dimension (15 minutes, set timer)

The purpose of this activity is to look at another dimension of the story and the special meaning it can have for us. The meeting of Mary and Elizabeth is a tender and deeply relational one. There are three moments in their meeting to consider in greater detail.

The first is Elizabeth's experience of inner joy. The child within her leaps for joy and she is filled with the Holy Spirit when she hears Mary's voice.

The second is Mary's experience of affirmation. Elizabeth's proclamation that Mary is the most blessed of all women and that her child is blessed affirms Mary's giftedness by God. No doubt Elizabeth's recognition of Mary as blessed (because she believed what she was told by the angel) is an assurance to Mary that all that she is experiencing is from God.

The third moment to consider is Mary's celebration of the power of God and a declaration of who she is. This is her great prayer which is known as the *Magnificat*, a name taken from the first word of the prayer in the Latin translation of the Bible.

So there is

·a filling of the Holy Spirit through the words of another person,

·the affirmation of one's experience with God, and

·the overflow into prayer from realizing the full import of what one has experienced.

Has there been a time when a person, a book, a movie, or an occurrence caused something to "leap within you"? Has there been a time when you *knew* something came as a gift from God?

I had such an experience while giving a conference in Nebraska. As I was talking with the participants after a morning presentation, a young man seated near the back of the room said in an off-hand manner, "I wonder if what we've been talking about relates to how we approach social justice in the church?" In that moment I felt a rush from the very center of my being, and two ideas with which I had been struggling for several months came together with great clarity. It was as if the last piece of a puzzle had been put into place. I could hardly contain myself as I shared this new grace of insight, and I ended by saying, "What a gift from God to me." Then looking at the young man who had made the comment, I said, "Thank you for being the word of God for me this morning!" He happily responded, "Amen."

Have there been times when your inner feelings—your *knowings*—were affirmed by someone?

Julia, a young mother of four children, shared a portion of her journal that expressed how she had been affirmed:

I've been thinking about getting back into writing. I've not written anything, not even a poem, since Joe (our second child) was born. It's been so long I really wondered if I still

76

had the talent and then even wondered if I was ever good at it anyway. I was standing at the sink and the phone rang. It was Susan, a college friend from whom I had not heard in ages. I don't believe what she said as her opening line to the conversation. This is a real gift. "Julia, I just had to call you. It's been a long time, but I was cleaning out some things and came across our college literary magazine and reread your short story that won you that scholarship money. I sat here and cried it was so beautiful. So I just had to call."

I believe that this was a call from God to affirm my own thoughts. We had a great talk and after I hung up, I went around singing at the top of my lungs and thanking God for this great gift.

Do you recall a time when, in the rush of feeling God's power within, you praised God in prayer or sang a favorite hymn? Mary and Elizabeth's unique encounter is an experience with which most of us can identify in some way.

Break/Rest/Body Movement (15 minutes)

If you are feeling tired and need to rest, set your timer before lying down. If you are going to walk or do other gentle body movement, keep track of the time with your watch. The purpose is to refresh yourself. Have a snack if you like, but whatever you do, continue to reflect in an easy way about the moment of encounter between Mary and Elizabeth.

Inner Dimension (30 minutes, set timer, get writing materials)

The purpose of this activity is to reflect on those moments from your past when God's power has been manifested in a Mary/Elizabeth experience.

Who have been Elizabeths to you—mentors or friends whose words or actions influenced your life? Who have been the people who caused you to feel "a movement within"? To whom have you been an Elizabeth? For whom have you been the mentor or friend who provided that word or action through which God enlivened them with the Holy Spirit?

Sometimes it is hard to imagine that we could be a vehicle of God's grace for another. Yet how often have people told us that they appreciated something we said or did. Sometimes we don't pay attention to those compliments or deny that we did anything of value. Now is a time to look back and consider moments when others have been the vehicle for bringing insights to you, and when you have done the same for others.

Make two lists.

1. Who Has Been an Elizabeth to Me? (As you enter names on this list, take a moment to reflect on your relationship to each person and how the situation affected you.)

·What was the insight or revelation that "leapt within" you?

·Was it an affirmation of your giftedness?

·Did it change you in some way?

·Did you celebrate the event in a prayer, song, or other creative way?

2. For Whom Have I Been an Elizabeth? (As you enter names on this list, take a moment to reflect about your relationship to each person and how you think the Holy Spirit was at work.)

·How did you affirm that person?

·What effect did your affirmation have?

·In affirming someone else, were you in some way affirmed yourself?

Prayer of Response (10 minutes, set timer)

The purpose of this activity is to allow God's creative word to move quietly within your mind and heart and body. Recall times of celebration and bask in those remembrances. Be still and return to this scripture (Psalm 46:8) whenever your attention wanders:

COME, SEE THE DEEDS OF THE MOST HIGH.

Reflection (10 minutes, set timer, get journaling materials)

Reflect on what you have discovered. You might want to write about or sketch a particularly powerful encounter that you recalled while making your two lists.

·Did you discover a pattern to the way you are affirmed and experience something new leaping within?

·Were there more women or men on your lists?

·Were the people you remembered mostly from a particular time in your life?

·Did you recall people or events that literally changed your life?

·What have you learned about yourself?

Close with Prayer (Or use the Lord's Prayer or one of the prayers or psalms from Part III)

O gracious God, I proclaim your greatness and your tender care. I thank you for the times when you have entered my life through those who serve as your messengers. I praise you for providing people through whom I have heard your word and felt something within me leap in joy. I thank you for those people who have heard your word through me. Empower me to continue hearing and speaking your word. *Amen.*

Overcoming Anxiety

"Therefore I tell you, do not worry about your life. . . ."

✳

Create the Environment (5 minutes)

Take a few minutes to create a comfortable environment for your time alone with God. What you do depends on whether you are indoors or out, at home or away. If you are inside, do whatever is necessary to avoid being interrupted by the telephone or the doorbell. Get comfortable within your space by turning away from anything distracting and by setting up whatever will help you get into a proper frame of mind. You may want to open your Bible and place it within easy reach next to some flowers or a candle.

Will a picture of Jesus, a cross, a crucifix, or an icon help make you more aware of God's presence? If so, place the item near the Bible or wherever you can easily look at it without being distracted. Have at hand everything you may need: notebook, drawing paper, pens, pencils, art materials.

The objective is to be settled before going further.

Open with Prayer

O God of all creation, I want to believe that you care for us always. But at times I feel anxious about what I have and what I want to have. Help me overcome my worries and realize that your loving care is ever present. I truly want to seek your kingdom first and to believe that all else will come to me as needed. *Amen.*

Be Still (10 minutes, set timer)

The purpose of these ten minutes is to relax the body and prepare the mind and heart to become more attentive as you enter into a special time alone with God. Some people do this by sitting quietly, while others find that gentle body movement is helpful. Often when we begin, our minds are cluttered and we feel distracted. Do not fight your thoughts or focus long on those that come to mind. Instead, breathe deeply and evenly as you reflect on scripture. Use a short prayer or this scripture (Psalm 121:5) as a touchstone, and come back to it over and over as you remain silent:

YAHWEH GUARDS YOU, SHADES YOU.

Read and Reflect on Scripture (25 minutes)

The story for this session (Matthew 6:25-34) is that of the birds of the air and the flowers of the field. Read the story over and over. You may like to read it quietly and then again out loud. There is great power in the spoken word, even when it is your voice and you are the audience. Think how the story applies to your life at this time. You have almost half an hour, so there is no need to rush. When something about the story strikes you, reflect on that idea. Be open to the Word, and allow God's Spirit to lead your thoughts.

> [And Jesus said,] "Therefore I tell you, do not worry about your life, what you will eat or what you will drink, or about your body, what you will wear. Is not life more than food, and the body more than clothing? Look at the birds of the air; they neither sow nor reap nor gather into barns, and yet your heavenly Father feeds them. Are you not of more value than they? And can any of you by worrying add a single hour to your span of life? And why do you worry about clothing? Consider the lilies of the field, how they grow; they neither toil nor spin, yet I tell you, even Solomon in all his glory was not clothed like one of these. But if God so clothes the grass of the field, which is alive today and tomorrow is thrown into the oven, will he not much more clothe you—you of little

faith? Therefore do not worry, saying, 'What will we eat?' or
'What will we drink?' or 'What will we wear?' For it is the
Gentiles who strive for all these things; and indeed your
heavenly Father knows that you need all these things. But
strive first for the kingdom of God and his righteousness, and
all these things will be given to you as well.

"So do not worry about tomorrow, for tomorrow will
bring worries of its own. Today's trouble is enough for
today."

Another Dimension (15 minutes, set timer)

This section of Matthew's Gospel is part of a larger dis-
course, or teaching, that Jesus gives, beginning with the beati-
tudes in Chapter 5. The Sermon on the Mount continues as
Jesus talks about the everyday living out of the Spirit. In the
passage we are considering, Jesus is talking to his followers
about detachment from things. Some people find this story
threatening, but I think of Jesus' words here as a friendly and
loving caution. When someone is overly worried about something, we are likely to comment, "Oh, just relax and it'll take
care of itself." We do not mean the person should do nothing;
we do mean the person should put things in their proper perspective. At this point in Matthew's Gospel, I believe that Jesus
was speaking in both a chiding and a loving way.

I especially like verse 34, where Jesus reminds us that we
should not be anxious about tomorrow. Does this mean we are
to ignore the future? Of course not. We are expected to deal
creatively with our life and our needs, but there are times
when we get so wrapped up in personal concerns that we lose
sight of what is truly important. We need to be reminded to
pay attention to the problem or situation at hand. While Jesus
is telling us to live in the now, this does not mean we are to
live only for today or in a hedonistic lifestyle. He calls for balance; he tells us to focus on what is important.

I think, for example, of two office workers who returned
from vacation to find their desks piled high with papers. One
bemoaned the work ahead and frittered time away, feeling

more anxious with every hour. The other set to work immediately, dividing the papers into three piles according to importance. While the first worker was still complaining and growing ever more anxious, the second had her priorities in order and was effectively getting on with the job at hand.

Now imagine yourself in the crowd of people looking up to where Jesus is standing a little above them on the hillside. As he speaks he makes use of what is around—birds flitting across the sky, flowers blossoming from the earth. He begins with a simple statement, "Do not worry . . . ."

People who begin to actively seek a deeper walk with God are often anxious about what is going to happen tomorrow, next week, next month. They cannot decide whether to pray or read scripture, get involved in good works, or go off alone to meditate. They are anxious to get *someplace* soon! Often they find it helpful to realize that there is not necessarily a place to get to, but there is a life to live in a purposeful way.

Break/Rest/Body Movement (15 minutes)

If you are feeling tired and need to rest, set your timer before lying down. If you are going for a walk or doing other gentle body movement, keep track of the time with your watch. The purpose of this activity is to refresh yourself. Have a snack if you like, but whatever you do, continue to reflect in an easy way on what Jesus said.

Inner Dimension (30 minutes, set timer, get writing materials)

Devote this time to examining your life to better understand what you may be anxious about. Also consider what steps to take to become more comfortable with your concerns.

Jesus mentioned five specific concerns: eating, drinking, the body, clothing, and tomorrow. To begin this activity, divide a sheet of paper into five columns:

Eating Drinking Body Clothing Tomorrow

Which of these do you worry about most? Print "1" over it. Which of these do you worry about least? Print "5" over it.

Now consider how anxious you are about the remaining topics and rank them "2," "3," and "4."

Fill the column under your #1 selection with personal thoughts about the topic. Be as specific as possible.

·When did I begin to be anxious?
·Can I name the anxiety?
·What is it doing to me physically? mentally?
·Is the problem more imagined than real?
·How have I tried to avoid the issue? resolve it?

It is important to learn as much as you can about whatever is causing you to feel anxious. Making specific notes will help you decide whether you are ready to take the actions needed to lower your level of anxiety and possibly remedy the situation.

Fill in all five columns if you like, but you may find it more helpful to limit your focus to only one or two areas of concern. Perhaps you will want to continue the exercise at some future time.

Many people think that money is the answer to all problems. Of course an adequate income is important, but beyond a certain point, more money will not help. In fact, money can lead us to become accumulators who never have enough possessions. Most of us are already accumulators to some extent. We have more shoes than we will ever need, or a closet full of clothes we do not wear, or a special drawer full of private possessions we think we cannot live without. We have compulsions to collect, to store away, and to hide. One woman I heard about was so in love with her possessions that she was actually buried in her favorite car.

Jesus makes it clear that those who attempt to walk in the spirit do not seek an abundance of material things. Often we need to be reminded that we are created in the image of God and are called to be sojourners. Because we have another home and are here only on a journey, we need only enough for our journey. Life is not a collection station; it is a time for living fully but simply. Anxieties and concerns will not leave us, but we must handle them as best we can and get on with life as Jesus would have us live it—simply.

Prayer of Response (10 minutes, set timer)
The purpose of this time is to free you of distractions and allow you to be more attentive to God moving quietly within your mind and heart. Some people like to sit in stillness. Others are drawn to let their body move in prayerful expression. As you sit in silence, return to this scripture (Psalm 146:9 RSV):
THE LORD WATCHES OVER THE SOJOURNERS.

Reflection (15 minutes, set timer, get journaling materials)
Now reflect on what God is revealing to you about those things that make you feel anxious. Look again at the thoughts you wrote during the Inner Dimension activity. Begin planning some simple changes in your life—changes that will help you overcome being anxious and to become more aware of being a sojourner, a traveler passing through this life. To get an idea of how others have approached this task, consider what Colleen, a mother of a newborn baby, wrote:

> I could identify so very well with this story. Ever since I can remember, I've been anxious about my appearance. I always worried about being too fat and spent way too much on clothes I didn't even wear. Then after I had the baby, I felt that he was getting all the attention and no one seemed to notice me any more.
> I realize now I'll never have the looks of a model. I need to accept myself the way I am, but there are some things I can do. I need to exercise more and change my eating habits. I must try to remember to ask God to free me from old ways of thinking.

Kathleen, a young artist, did not come up with any special idea about what she might do to change her life. Instead, she confronted a question that made her reconsider her worth. Showing me her bright colored sketch of a rose, she said, "I guess that because I'm a painter I see things that a lot of people don't. I love to do flowers, and I really did identify with Jesus' statement that even Solomon in his glory was not like one of these. Just to sit and look at the intricate designs in a flower is enough to awe me. And I wonder, Am I worth even more than that flower?"

Use the remaining time to think about what God is helping you to realize about yourself. Express your thoughts in words or art so you will have something to look back on to see how you are growing spiritually.

·From what anxieties would I like to be freed?

·What steps can I take to bring more peace into my life?

Close with Prayer (Or use the Lord's Prayer or one of the prayers or psalms from Part III)

O God, help me to understand that I am only on a journey here in this world. When my days get cluttered and I feel anxious, show me ways to simplify my life. Help me to recognize how the quest for material possessions can become an obsession. Open my eyes to everything in nature that is wonder-full, so that I may be reminded of Jesus' teaching that I am worth more than all of that. I pray in Jesus' name. *Amen.*

Turning Around
"What am I to do?"

✳

Create the Environment (5 minutes)

Take a few minutes to create a comfortable environment for your time alone. What you do depends on whether you are indoors or out, at home or away. If you are inside, do whatever is necessary to avoid being interrupted by the telephone or doorbell. Get comfortable in the space by turning away from anything distracting and by setting up whatever will help you get into a proper frame of mind. You may want to open your Bible and place it next to a candle or flowers.

Will a picture of Jesus, a cross, a crucifix, or an icon help make you more aware of God's presence? If so, place the item near the Bible or wherever you can easily look at it without being distracted. Have at hand everything you may need: notebook, drawing paper, pens, pencils, art materials.

The objective is to be settled before going further.

Open with Prayer

O God, I thank you for sending Jesus into this world. I want to believe and to serve as Jesus commanded, but I have moments of doubt and weakness. Help me to review what I believe and to become aware of ways I must change in order to serve others more faithfully. Guide me to a deeper understanding of whatever needs to be turned around in my life. *Amen.*

Be Still (10 minutes, set timer)

The purpose of these ten minutes is to relax the body and prepare the mind and heart to become more attentive as you enter into a special time alone with God. Some people do this by sitting quietly, while others find that gentle body movement is helpful. Often when we begin, our minds are cluttered and we feel distracted. Do not fight your thoughts or focus long on those that come to mind. Instead, breathe deeply and evenly as you reflect on scripture. Use this scripture (Psalm 38:21) as a touchstone, and come back to it over and over as you remain silent:

O MY GOD, BE NOT FAR FROM ME!

Read and Reflect on Scripture (25 minutes, set timer)

The story for this session (Acts 22:3-16) is that of Saul's experience on the road to Damascus.

Read the story over and over. You may like to read it quietly and then again out loud. There is great power in the spoken word, even when it is your voice and you are the audience. You have almost half an hour, so there is no need to rush. When something about the story strikes you, reflect on that idea. Be open to the Word and allow God's Spirit to lead your thoughts.

[Saul says,] "I am a Jew, born at Tarsus in Cilicia, but brought up in this city at the feet of Gamaliel, educated strictly according to our ancestral law, being zealous for God, just as all of you are today. I persecuted this Way up to the point of death by binding both men and women and putting them in prison, as the high priest and the whole council of elders can testify about me. From them I also received letters to the brothers in Damascus, and I went there in order to bind those who were there and to bring them back to Jerusalem for punishment.

"While I was on my way and approaching Damascus, about noon a great light from heaven suddenly shone about me. I fell to the ground and heard a voice saying to me, 'Saul,

Saul, why are you persecuting me?' I answered, 'Who are you, Lord?' Then he said to me, 'I am Jesus of Nazareth whom you are persecuting.' Now those who were with me saw the light but did not hear the voice of the one who was speaking to me. I asked, 'What am I to do, Lord?' The Lord said to me, 'Get up and go to Damascus; there you will be told everything that has been assigned to you to do.' Since I could not see because of the brightness of that light, those who were with me took my hand and led me to Damascus.

"A certain Ananias, who was a devout man according to the law and well spoken of by all the Jews living there, came to me; and standing beside me, he said, 'Brother Saul, regain your sight!' In that very hour I regained my sight and saw him. Then he said, 'The God of our ancestors has chosen you to know his will, to see the Righteous One and to hear his own voice; for you will be his witness to all the world of what you have seen and heard. And now why do you delay? Get up, be baptized, and have your sins washed away, calling on his name.'"

Another Dimension (15 minutes, set timer)

The purpose of this activity is to look at another dimension of the story.

The Acts of the Apostles includes two tellings (Chapters 9 and 22) of the story of Paul's conversion experience. The story is first told in a factual style we might expect to find in a newspaper report of the event. I find the second telling to be more helpful because it is a personal account that Paul uses in speaking before an audience.

What does Paul reveal about himself through his own account? He has reflected on his experience and recognizes that it is the foundation of both his ministry and his view of life in Jesus. This is an honest and straightforward testimony. Without fanfare or exaggeration, Paul tells who he is and what has happened to him. He offers no apologies for his past, but neither does he make himself out to be worse than he was. Paul makes it clear that he was acting out of ignorance and was not guilty of purposely doing anything against God.

Despite Paul's zealous actions, he did not have a closed mind and was receptive to new ideas. We see how the question "Saul, Saul, why are you persecuting me?" opened a whole new world, instead of leading to an argument or another defensive measure.

Paul [as Saul] had questions of his own. "Who are you, Lord?" he asks. Then comes the statement that compels Paul throughout his life: "I am Jesus of Nazareth whom you are persecuting."

Again, there is an honest and touching response: "What am I to do, Lord?" The question helps us understand just how open Paul was to whatever God had to say.

At this point we might consider what our reaction would have been. Often when we feel that God has spoken to us, we quickly decide on a course of action rather than waiting quietly for confirmation.

Paul's conversion experience involved not only a turning point in his life, but also a profound insight into the meaning of community. Although Paul was zealous for God both before and after the experience that began on the road to Damascus, he changed in an important way. He came to realize that those he had been persecuting were his companions in faith. We, too, can turn about from our old ways of thinking and acting to become more open to hearing God identify with persecuted people.

Break/Rest/Body Movement (15 minutes)

If you are feeling tired and need to rest, set your timer before lying down. If you are going for a walk or doing other gentle body movement, keep track of the time with your watch. The purpose of this activity is to refresh yourself. Have a snack if you like, but whatever you do, continue to reflect in an easy way about Paul's experience.

Inner Dimension (30 minutes, set timer, get writing materials)

The purpose of this activity is to consider what we might be doing that is "putting people down" without our realizing it. We have seen that Saul, in his zeal, was persecuting others. It required a dramatic encounter for him to realize that he must change his ways.

Print these words at the top of a sheet of paper:

    Family   Friends   Groups/Organizations

Now examine your actions and attitudes. Begin by considering your relationships within your immediate family. Perhaps some behavior that seems not only reasonable but good to you needs to be "turned around." Think especially of those things you are doing or saying to others that you believe are "for their own good." Is it really the loving behavior you think it is? Make notes to yourself under all three columns.

Review your actions and attitudes carefully, keeping in mind Saul's hurtful zeal. We should question anything we are doing expressly "for the good of others"; it may be a form of oppression.

Prayer of Response (10 minutes, set timer)

The purpose of this time is to free you of distractions and allow you to be more attentive to God moving quietly within your mind and heart. Some people like to sit in stillness. Others are drawn to let their body move in prayerful expression. Whenever your attention wanders, return to this scripture (Psalm 54:2):

O GOD, HEAR MY PRAYER.

Reflection (15 minutes, set timer, get journaling materials)

Now reflect on those habits and beliefs you might be required to turnabout in order to experience a breakthrough in your spiritual life. What you write or draw in your notebook or journal must be personal and honest. To get an idea of how others have approached this task, consider the reflections of Laurie. She was in her late teens and attending a technical school when she wrote:

> Every time I hear the story about Saul on the road to Damascus, I'm reminded of the way I grew up thinking about religion. My parents always gave me the impression that our church was *the* church. They never really said it, but I got the impression that we were better Christians than the people who belonged to other churches. It was like we were the chosen ones.
>
> Then I went away to school and met lots of new people. Most of them came from other Christian denominations. Even though they seemed to practice their faith sincerely, I realize now that I did feel a little superior to them. I sort of let that idea float to the back of my mind. But now as I write about it, I see that I've got to do a lot of rethinking. I truly need to turn around from being so proud.

Jan had a private consulting business that demanded a lot of travel. She chose to sketch a picture to express her insights from this experience. The picture was in three sections. In one section there was a large office building. The second section had a picture of a large car. In the third section there was a tiny house and three little people standing by it. As Jan looked at her sketch, she realized that her home and family had become secondary in her life. This made her aware of the turnabout to which God was calling her.

Sam was a sales rep approaching retirement. He held onto his way of doing things like a dog hanging onto a bone. There was only one way to look at any question, and that was Sam's way. It got so bad that he almost lost his job and his family. But finally Sam had a breakthrough experience that turned his life around. This is what he wrote:

> I truly believed that if someone had not had my experience they *could not* be a real Christian. Paul's story helped me see

that my problem was that I hadn't heard Jesus say, "Go and wait till I send someone to you." I went off preaching and proclaiming as if I knew it all.

Sam came to realize that he needed some quiet time to reconsider how Jesus was calling him. The turnabout came slowly, but Sam made it and in time became a much humbler man.

Now it is your turn to express yourself. Reread what you wrote during the Inner Dimension activity.

·What is God helping me to see about myself today?

·What behavior might God be calling me to turn from?

·Have I been blind to some aspect of my life that needs changing?

·How might I be called to make a breakthrough in some personal relationship?

Be as specific as possible, and try to think of three things you can begin to do immediately to continue growing in God's power and grace.

Close with Prayer (Or use the Lord's Prayer or one of the prayers or psalms from Part III)

O God of all creation, I thank you for life and for the chance to turnabout on whatever paths are not best for me. I have reviewed my everyday habits. Grant me the strength to turn around whenever necessary and to seek a better path. I realize that I do not always see you in other people. Please fill me with power to understand the attitudes of others and to discover what is holy in them. I want to heal differences of opinion and live rightly. *Amen.*

Called to Serve

"So come, I will send you to Pharaoh to bring my people,
the Israelites, out of Egypt."

✳

Create the Environment (5 minutes)

Take a few minutes to create a comfortable environment
for your time alone with God. What you do depends on
whether you are indoors or out, at home or away. If you are
inside, do whatever is necessary to avoid being interrupted by
the telephone or the doorbell. Get comfortable within your
space by turning away from anything distracting and by
setting up whatever will help you get into a proper frame of
mind. You may want to open your Bible and place it within
easy reach next to some flowers or a candle.

Will a picture of Jesus, a cross, a crucifix, or an icon help
make you more aware of God's presence? If so, place the item
near the Bible or wherever you can easily look at it without
being distracted. Have at hand everything you may need:
notebook, drawing paper, pens, pencils, art materials.

The objective is to be settled before going further.

Open with Prayer

God, I have put aside this time to be alone with you. I come
away from my daily routine with a wish to be on holy ground
and sense your presence in my life in a new way. Help me to
hear your voice during this time and come to a better
understanding of the ministry to which I am called. *Amen.*

Be Still (10 minutes, set timer)

The purpose of these ten minutes is to relax the body and prepare the mind and heart to become more attentive as you enter into a special time alone with God. Some people do this by sitting quietly, while others find that gentle body movement is helpful. Often when we begin, our minds are cluttered and we feel distracted. Do not fight your thoughts or focus long on those that come to mind. Instead, breathe deeply and evenly as you reflect on scripture. Use this scripture (Psalm 25:2) as a touchstone, and come back to it over and over as you remain silent:

O MY GOD, IN YOU I TRUST.

Read and Reflect on Scripture (25 minutes, set timer)

For this session we look back to a story from the Hebrew Scriptures that speaks dramatically about God's voice in our lives. The story of the burning bush is found in Exodus 3:1-12. Read the story over and over. You may like to read it quietly and again out loud. There is great power in the spoken word, even when it is your voice and you are the audience. You have almost half an hour, so there is no need to rush. When something about the story strikes you, reflect on that idea. Be open to the Word and allow God to lead your thoughts.

Moses was keeping the flock of his father-in-law Jethro, the priest of Midian; he led his flock beyond the wilderness, and came to Horeb, the mountain of God. There the angel of the Lord appeared to him in a flame of fire out of a bush; he looked, and the bush was blazing, yet it was not consumed. Then Moses said, "I must turn aside and look at this great sight, and see why the bush is not burned up." When the Lord saw that he had turned aside to see, God called to him out of the bush, "Moses, Moses!" And he said, "Here I am." Then he said, "Come no closer! Remove the sandals from your feet, for the place on which you are standing is holy ground." He said further, "I am the God of your father, the

God of Abraham, the God of Isaac, and the God of Jacob."
And Moses hid his face for he was afraid to look at God.

Then the Lord said, "I have observed the misery of my
people who are in Egypt; I have heard their cry on account of
their taskmasters. Indeed, I know their sufferings, and I have
come down to deliver them from the Egyptians, and to bring
them up out of that land to a good and broad land, a land
flowing with milk and honey, to the country of the
Canaanites, the Hittites, the Amorites, the Perizzites, the
Hivites, and the Jebusites. The cry of the Israelites has now
come to me; I have also seen how the Egyptians oppress
them. So come, I will send you to Pharaoh to bring my people,
the Israelites, out of Egypt." But Moses said to God, "Who am
I that I should go to Pharaoh, and bring the Israelites out of
Egypt?" He said, "I will be with you; and this shall be the sign
for you that it is I who sent you: when you have brought the
people out of Egypt, you shall worship God on this mountain."

Another Dimension (15 minutes, set timer)

The purpose of this activity is to look at another dimension
of the story. In this case, we will consider how the events
Moses experienced can help us understand what God reveals
for us today. There is a pattern we can identify.

God calls us away from where we are. Usually God attracts
our attention with something out of the ordinary. Our
"burning bush" may be an event, a person, a statement, or
even an unusual thought. What catches us is something or
someone that touches us so deeply we cannot shake it off.

*We recognize that something is different and sense that it de-
mands our pursuit on a personal level.* The unusual event that
captured our attention has an aura of mystery that demands
investigation and an explanation. Nowadays, we have such a
yearning to understand or tendency to explain away
everything that we are in danger of losing our appreciation of
the mysterious and the need for it in our lives.

We hear a call. Hearing the call does not necessarily mean we will hear it with our ears, although we might. We may hear God's call with our intuitive sense, through a dream, or in some other way. Most of us have fewer and fewer moments of quiet reflection, and some young people are so plugged into sound that they may have completely lost the ability to listen for anything mysterious. It is important to be attentive so as not to lose our ability to recognize and appreciate the mysterious.

We answer. We can, of course, ignore everything about the burning bush experience, but some aspect of it will come back to us. It may be that we, like Moses, hide our face when we recognize that we are in God's presence. Eventually, though, Moses responded to the call. Can we do less?

Finally, we receive a commission to ministry. The experience of the burning bush is always a commission to do something with or for others. It is a mistake to consider the experience as being for us alone.

For those trying to find a way through their own burning bush encounters, God's call to ministry has always been a calling forth of strengths or skills acquired in the past. That is, everything that has happened up to the time of the call is necessary preparation. If we look again to Moses, we see that his knowledge of both the Hebrew and Egyptian worlds suited him for the task ahead. It is the same with us.

If you have time, reread the story with these ideas in mind.

Break/Rest/Body Movement (15 minutes)

If you are feeling tired and need to rest, set your timer before lying down. If you are going for a walk or doing other gentle body movement, keep track of the time with your watch. The purpose of this activity is to refresh yourself. Have a snack if you like, but whatever you do, continue to reflect in an easy way about the story of Moses and the burning bush.

Inner Dimension (30 minutes, set timer)

The purpose of this activity is to review your own life to better understand what God has been preparing you for.

Every one of us has a story to tell about a burning bush. Perhaps you are already thinking about a particular experience in your life and are ready to put it on paper. Or maybe you feel the need to ponder awhile. In either case, it is helpful to see examples from the lives of others.

Martin had been ordained for a number of years. Everything was going well for him, yet he had an unease that led him to the experience he talks about here:

> I guess I've come to learn that whenever I get to feeling a little uncomfortable, that's a sign to be alert. One day I was reading in a church magazine and found myself going through the Positions Wanted & Needed section. I didn't remember ever having read that section before, but there I was giving it full attention. All of a sudden one four-line ad appeared like a neon sign. It shocked me so that I put the magazine aside.
>
> An hour later I came back to the ad, and it was like the letters were four feet tall! Needless to say, I applied for the position and got it. I see now that it was exactly what I had been preparing for for years. I haven't told this to many people, because I'm sure they'd think I was looney.

Donna, a mother of teenagers, had a similar experience, but in her case it was brought about by another person.

> I was at a weekend retreat and everything was going well. Then out of the blue I was handed a note from someone I knew at home. She said she was praying for me while I was on retreat. As I read that note, it was like a fire consuming me. I couldn't understand what was happening. It was as though a whole new world of God's power opened up to me. I was struck with awe and began crying joyfully. I recognized that I was on holy ground.

Accustomed to working under pressure as a business consultant, John had not thought much about his spiritual life. When he became aware of the idea that we have all had a burning bush experience, he became more attentive to the possibility that God's time and our time do indeed intersect. John explained:

> I was overseeing a conference of five people who got into a heated discussion. It was my job to observe the process in order to reflect back to them some of the causes of their office problems. One of the men suddenly said, "I don't want to talk about it any more. We're getting nowhere."
>
> There was an embarrassing silence.
>
> I had an immediate awareness that there was a power present that I couldn't explain. I heard myself saying, "I have a sense we're on holy ground. And in the midst of the mystery of trying to understand the problem, we're nearly at the resolution and the revelation of it."
>
> It was odd. I'd never said anything like that before. The others looked at me and seemed to sense something different at that moment as well. A resolution came quickly after that. God's power was at work in my work.

Melanie drew what appeared to be a stained glass burning bush with her face in the middle of it and flames coming out of her ears. She interpreted it by saying there had been a time when she had "heard" someone pay her a compliment that she had yearned to hear since she was a little child.

* * *

Now get out your journaling materials.

Spend the remainder of your time recalling a moment in your life when you felt you were on holy ground, a moment when you were having a burning bush experience.

·When did it happen?

·What was your immediate reaction?

·How do you feel about the experience now?

Prayer of Response (10 minutes, set timer)

The purpose of this time is to free you of distractions and allow you to be more attentive to God moving quietly within your mind and heart. Some people like to sit in stillness. Others are drawn to let their body move in prayerful expression. Whenever your attention wanders, return to this scripture (Psalm 111:1):

I WILL THANK YOU, YAHWEH,

WITH ALL MY HEART.

Reflection (10 minutes, set timer, get writing materials)

Now review the special moment, or moments, when you felt you were on holy ground. See if you can discover to what you have been called.

Although the direction may not be immediately clear, each experience of being on holy ground is an invitation to minister to others in some way. Remember that through our baptism, we are all called to be ministers. However, many people have used the term "minister" to refer only to those who are ordained, when in fact we are all called to ministry. Larry, a former drinker who now counsels other alcoholics, wrote:

> I didn't know what I wanted to do with my life. I drifted from one job to another, and it seemed the only thing I knew how to do well was drink. As the years went on, it reached the point where just about everybody gave up on me.
>
> I see now that even the worst things that happened to me can have some value. God had something useful for me to do. I was just too stubborn to see that for a long, long time.
>
> It's still a revelation to me that God should be so patient!

Now it is your turn to express yourself. What has God been revealing to you that you can now admit to yourself? Are you called to head a group? Adopt a problem child? Join a cause? Teach someone to read? Turn your back on a destructive behavior and use your experience to help others? Is God telling you to change your profession? Renew your commitment to your marriage?

God is calling, but only you can answer. Look deeply and honestly at yourself. Make notes in your journal, and outline the steps you know you should take in response to the burning bush experience, or experiences, in your life.

Close with Prayer (Or use the Lord's Prayer or one of the prayers or psalms from Part III)

O God, I realize that you called Moses at a time when he least expected it. Is the same thing happening to me? As I grow older, I want to understand what you have been preparing me for. Help me to be aware of the holy ground you place before me. Open my ears that I may hear, and open my heart to embrace the ministry to which you call me. *Amen.*

Making the Crooked Straight

"When Jesus saw her he called her over."

✳

Create the Environment (5 minutes)

Take a few minutes to create a comfortable environment for your time alone. What you do depends on whether you are indoors or out, at home or away. If you are inside, do whatever is necessary to avoid being interrupted by the telephone or doorbell. Get comfortable in the space by turning away from anything distracting and by setting up whatever will help you get into a proper frame of mind. You may want to open your Bible and place it next to a candle or flowers.

Will a picture of Jesus, a cross, a crucifix, or an icon help make you more aware of God's presence? If there is something that will help you focus your attention, place the item near the Bible or wherever you can easily look at it without being distracted. Before going on, have at hand everything you may need: notebook, drawing paper, pens, pencils, art materials.

The objective is to be settled before going further.

Open with Prayer

O God, prepare my mind and heart to accept a new understanding of my worth as I enter into a time of prayer. Help me to recognize what it means to be your child and accept the life you have called me to lead. I open myself to your Spirit. Lead me in honesty and truth that I may hear the words of Jesus. *Amen.*

Be Still (10 minutes, set timer)

The purpose of these ten minutes is to relax the body and prepare the mind and heart to become more attentive as you enter into a special time alone with God. Some people do this by sitting quietly, while others find that gentle body movement is helpful. Often when we begin, our minds are cluttered and we feel distracted. Do not fight your thoughts or focus long on those that come to mind. Instead, breathe deeply and evenly as you reflect on scripture. Use a short prayer or this scripture (Psalm 29:4) as a touchstone, and come back to it over and over as you remain silent:

THE VOICE OF GOD IS POWERFUL.

Read and Reflect on Scripture, (25 minutes, set timer)

The story for this session (Luke 13:10-17) is that of the woman who, after living with an affliction for eighteen years, was healed of her infirmity. Read the story over and over. You may like to read it quietly and then again out loud. There is power in the spoken word, even when it is your voice and you are the audience. You have almost half an hour, so you need not rush. When something strikes you, reflect on that idea. Be open and allow God's Spirit to lead your thoughts.

Now he [Jesus] was teaching in one of the synagogues on the sabbath. And just then there appeared a woman with a spirit that had crippled her for eighteen years. She was bent over and was quite unable to stand up straight. When Jesus saw her, he called her over and said, "Woman, you are set free from your ailment." When he laid his hands on her, immediately she stood up straight and began praising God. But the leader of the synagogue, indignant because Jesus had cured on the sabbath, kept saying to the crowd, "There are six days on which work ought to be done; come on those days and be cured, and not on the sabbath day." But the Lord answered him and said, "You hypocrites! Does not each of you on the sabbath untie his ox or his donkey from the manger, and lead it away to give it water? And ought not this woman, a daughter of Abraham whom Satan bound for eighteen long years, be set free from this bondage on the sabbath day?" When he said this, all his opponents were put to shame; and the entire crowd was rejoicing at all the wonderful things that he was doing.

Another Dimension (15 minutes, set timer)

The purpose of this activity is to look at another dimension of the story and the special meaning it can have for us. Three historical facts are important to understanding the passage:

1. At this time in history, the prevailing belief was that sickness, especially a deformity, resulted from having sinned and that demons were present. A rabbi who touched someone such as the woman in this story (a sinner and therefore unclean) would himself become unclean.

2. Jesus refers to the unnamed woman as a "daughter of Abraham," a rare expression identifying her as one of the faithful people of God. The term, which is not found anywhere else in the Christian Testament, is a unique sign of dignity.

3. Leaders of this synagogue community and sabbath laws did not permit work on the sabbath. And healing was considered work. The story shows how Jesus, in healing the woman, is clearly challenging the exclusive, legalistic mindset of the religious leaders. The fact that Jesus touches this woman shows that his compassion and healing extend to all, even the lowly and outcast. His totally inclusive mindset creates a sense of awe and wonder among the ordinary people.

Break/Rest/Body Movement (15 minutes)

If you are feeling tired and need to rest, set your timer before lying down. If you are going to walk or do other gentle body movement, keep track of the time with your watch.

The purpose of this activity is to refresh yourself. Have a snack if you like, but whatever you do, continue to reflect in an easy way about the story of the woman Jesus calls "a daughter of Abraham" and how her encounter with Jesus speaks to you.

Inner Dimension (30 minutes, set timer, get writing materials)
The purpose of this activity is to look at how Jesus calls to you and offers release from affliction. The woman in the story was freed of a physical affliction that she had lived with for eighteen years. Many of us are afflicted not in our body, but in our mind and in our spirit. Such afflictions may manifest themselves as addictions, compulsions, or other dysfunctional behaviors. It is possible to be as disabled emotionally and spiritually as the bent-over woman was disabled physically.

After reflecting on the scripture passage, Florence, a single woman in her thirties, remembered abusive situations from her past and made this journal entry:

> I realize more and more it seems that I have been made crooked over the years. I knew that I had to look at things in a different way and always be sure that I was on balance. I think that I am now able to listen for a call to healing. It's amazing that I have felt so untouchable. I have felt dirty. But the amazing thing is that nothing is dirty to God. God has reached into the untouchable places in my life and I am being healed by that touch.

Steven was a priest in his early fifties when he reflected on this story during a time of prayer. He saw patterns in his life that needed healing and described his insight this way:

> My anger and distancing were the spirits that bent me over throughout these years. I yearned to belong. I talked about community and yet never felt like I was a part of the community. And I know people were repulsed by my anger and distanced by my distancing.
> Today in the prayer time I imagined Jesus teaching in my church and calling me from the seat at the side of the sanctuary. As I stood in front of him, I was looking at his feet because I was bent over. It dawned on me that maybe I never had looked him in the face. And then I felt him touch me . . . .

Think about how you are in some way like the woman in the story who lived with her affliction for so many years. Consider ways your mind or spirit has been crippled. Reflect on these questions, and record your thoughts in your journal.

·Are patterns of behavior or issues of life weighing heavily on me?

·What in my life leaves me feeling outcast or unclean?

·What aspect of my life is most in need of healing?

Listen for God's voice. Perhaps it will come through words Jesus spoke or through someone who at one time told you what you needed to hear. Let God remove your burden and empower you to stand straight and tall. God's touch can give you a new-found dignity.

Prayer of Response (10 minutes, set timer)

The purpose of this time is to become more aware of God's healing power. Reflect on what you have written and how God has touched your life. Whenever your attention wanders, be still and return to this scripture (Psalm 107:20):

GOD SENT A WORD TO HEAL THEM.

Reflection (10 minutes, set timer, get journaling materials)

Now reflect on what you have discovered about yourself, and how God has touched you during this time. Write about, or illustrate, an experience of healing that helped you regain you dignity and stand tall once more.

Close with Prayer (Or use the Lord's Prayer or one of the prayers or psalms from Part III)

I thank you, God, for calling me to come to you. Once again I have been touched by your power and tenderness. Guide me to follow your ways and to experience the dignity that comes with knowing I am your child. Continue to reveal to me those painful places in my life. When I am hurting in mind or spirit, grant me the grace to come to you for healing. *Amen.*

Grief into Joy
"Woman, why are you weeping?"

∗

Create the Environment (5 minutes)

Create a comfortable environment for your time alone. What you do depends on whether you are indoors or out, at home or away. If you are inside, do whatever is necessary to avoid being interrupted by the telephone or doorbell. Get comfortable in the space by turning away from anything distracting and by setting up whatever will help you get into a proper frame of mind. You may want to open your Bible and place it next to a candle or flowers.

Will a picture of Jesus, a cross, a crucifix, or an icon help make you more aware of God's presence? If there is something that will help you focus your attention, place the item near the Bible or wherever you can easily look at it without being distracted. Before going on, have at hand everything you may need: notebook, drawing paper, pens, pencils, art materials.

The objective is to be settled before going further.

Open with Prayer

O God, there have been times when grief has overtaken me, times when things were confused and I could not understand. I come to you as a child to a loving parent. Help me to understand that grief is part of life and that I can move through it and again know joy. May joy beyond my expectation be revealed to me as Jesus revealed joy to Mary. *Amen.*

Be Still (10 minutes, set timer)

The purpose of these ten minutes is to relax the body and prepare the mind and heart to become more attentive as you enter into a special time alone with God. Some people do this by sitting quietly, while others find that gentle body movement is helpful. Often when we begin, our minds are cluttered and we feel distracted. Do not fight your thoughts or focus long on those that come to mind. Instead, breathe deeply and evenly as you reflect on scripture. Use a short prayer or this scripture (Psalm 46:1) as a touchstone, and come back to it over and over as you remain silent:

GOD IS OUR REFUGE AND OUR STRENGTH.

Read and Reflect on Scripture (25 minutes, set timer)

The story for this session (John 20:11-18) is that of Mary of Magdala at the tomb of Jesus. Read the story over and over. You may want to read it to yourself and then out loud. There is great power in the spoken word, even when it is your voice and you are the audience. Consider how you are in some way like each of the characters in the story. You have almost half an hour to do this, so there is no need to rush. When something about the story strikes you, reflect on that idea. Be open to the Word and allow God's Spirit to guide your thoughts.

> But Mary stood weeping outside the tomb. As she wept, she bent over to look into the tomb; and she saw two angels in white, sitting where the body of Jesus had been lying, one at the head and the other at the feet. They said to her, "Woman, why are you weeping?" She said to them, "They have taken away my Lord, and I do not know where they have laid him." When she had said this, she turned around and saw Jesus standing there, but she did not know that it was Jesus. Jesus said to her, "Woman why are you weeping? Whom are you looking for?" Supposing him to be the gardener, she said to him, "Sir, if you have carried him away, tell me where you have laid him, and I will take him away." Jesus said to her, "Mary!" She turned and said to him in Hebrew, "Rab-boni!"

(which means Teacher). Jesus said to her, "Do not hold on to me, because I have not yet ascended to the Father. But go to my brothers and say to them, 'I am ascending to my Father and your Father, to my God and your God.'" Mary Magdalene went and announced to the disciples, "I have seen the Lord;" and she told them that he had said these things to her.

Another Dimension (15 minutes, set timer)

Our purpose is to look at another dimension of the story. Mary Magdalene, who comes to the tomb when it is still dark and finds the stone has been moved away, hurries to tell Peter and John. They come running to the tomb. Finding only the clothes in which Jesus had been buried, Peter and John return to their homes. Mary, however, stays at the tomb weeping.

In John's telling of the resurrection story, Mary sees the angels dressed in white and sitting where the body of Jesus had lain. Because of the climate and environment, no mortal would be wearing white clothes. In the tradition of the time, saying someone was dressed in white was to say that God's power was present, as in the Transfiguration of Jesus (Luke 9:29), where Jesus' clothes became "dazzling white." Clearly, John's message in this gospel reading is that God's power of life is present in the tomb, the symbol of death and loss.

It is interesting to note that Mary is asked the same question twice; first by the angels, and then by Jesus: "Woman, why are you crying?" It seems obvious that Mary's tears were an expression of her grief and the confusion she felt over the loss of Jesus. Unlike Mary, when we first experience a loss, we may be too stunned to cry. But at some point the tears begin to fall, and it seems they will never stop. There appears to be no end to our crying.

Sam was a sales executive in his forties when his best friend was killed in a boating accident. He asked to see me, and as we sat talking, tears welled up in his eyes. "It's been six months since Julian died," he said, "and people don't understand how I can still feel so bad about it. They think I should be over my loss by now. I guess I need to know if it's normal to grieve this long."

Over the years I have learned that there is no timetable for grief. We each experience loss and sorrow in our own way. I told Sam that what he was going through was normal and natural, and that by acknowledging his feelings and finding ways to deal with them, his grief would lessen and pass. Even though it was hard for Sam to believe so at the time, I assured him that joy would again have a place in his life. "In your pain and confusion, Sam, look for Jesus and listen for his voice," I said. "He is there for you and often you will find him in the kindness and help of friends, family, and even strangers."

So often we are unaware of Jesus' presence in our lives. In the midst of Mary Magdalene's grief he appeared to her, but she did not recognize him. Likewise, in the midst of our own pain, we are sometimes unable to see that God is with us and will help us work through our grief to a renewed sense of joy.

Break/Rest/Body Movement (15 minutes)

If you are feeling tired and need to rest, set your timer before lying down. If you are going for a walk or doing other gentle body movement, keep track of the time with your watch. The purpose of this activity is to refresh yourself. Have a snack if you like, but whatever you do, continue to reflect in an easy way on the story of Mary meeting Jesus at the tomb.

Inner Dimension (30 minutes, set timer, get writing materials)

The purpose of this activity is to review the ways in which you have experienced healing in your life.

At the top of your paper make a column for these headings:

LOSS   POINT OF HEALING   NEW LIFE

In the first column, list times when you felt that all was lost: death of a loved one, divorce, loss of a job, experiences of betrayal or rejection.

In the second column, note the point at which healing began. Consider how God was present to you in that experience: through friends, family, support groups, church, insights. Remember, when we are in the midst of a situation, we often fail to see what is obvious in hindsight. Don't be hard on yourself if you were not aware of God's presence at the time.

In the third column, write and reflect on the insights and new growth that have come as a result of the healing process.

During a retreat, Susan wrote the following after reflecting on the scripture of Mary Magdalene at the tomb of Jesus:

Last Friday morning I guess I passed a milestone. One of the women at work confided in me today that she was going through a divorce. She started to cry and was afraid she would just fall apart in my office and not be able to continue the day. I saw myself sitting in front of me. It was a funny feeling. I felt God's presence there between us in a very strong way, and I heard myself saying things that I never would have thought I would be able to say. I talked about how everything she was feeling was good and natural. I didn't preach, but I was aware that I have healed. It's not that I have seen so much good come out of that horrible experience of mine, but it is that I can give a message of hope simply by being. I have heard God call my name and I have seen a new life. In fact, I went back and reread my journal from six months ago and found two entries which really show the loss and deep grief and the healing point in my life. The first is right after my divorce:

June 22. Here I am—35 and single again. I feel like my life has ended. I feel confused and lonely. How do I erase 14 years of a relationship? Where is God in all this? I don't know whether I will survive. All my hopes have been dashed and ruined.

The other entry is at Christmastime:

December 23. Today I visited Jane whose husband died last week. It's strange, but I found it so healing for me. She thanks me for understanding her loss and letting her cry— and especially for crying with her.

As you recall your own experiences of loss, reflect on how God has been, and is now, with you.

Prayer of Response (10 minutes, set timer)
    This time is to increase your awareness of how God has been present as you moved from grief into joy. Look over what you have written. It speaks of your walk with God and how, if you are open, new life can emerge from loss. When your attention wanders, return to this scripture (Psalm 66:5):
    COME AND SEE WHAT GOD HAS DONE.

Reflection (10 minutes, set timer, get writing materials)
    Now reflect on what you have discovered about yourself.
    ·Did a pattern emerge as to how healing takes place in your life?
    ·Does healing come through others?
    ·Has prayer been helpful for you during times of loss?
    ·How has new life emerged out of your grief? Many find when they reach out to others, their own lives begin to heal.
    ·In what ways can your experience of pain and growth beyond it be a foundation for a ministry to someone else?

Close with Prayer (Or use the Lord's Prayer or one of the prayers or psalms from Part III)
    Thank you, God of creation, for breathing life into the earth. Thank you for bringing order out of chaos. Again and again you have been present to me in the midst of grief and confusion. You call me by name and let me see the new life your Spirit calls forth from the chaos. Continue the healing you have begun in me, and let me be a witness to others of your healing love. *Amen.*

Prayers

This section contains prayers you may use in place of those written into the sessions or as prayers throughout the day.

We all have our individual ways of praying just as we have our individual ways of talking. I have included prayers and psalms to help you, whether you are accustomed to speaking with God formally or informally. Some of the prayers are meant to be used at specific times, such as morning, noon, evening, and end of the day. Others may be used whenever they seem suitable.

Christian history includes a tradition of praying several times during the day. In the past, when the rhythm of life was more set, prayer patterns were also more set. People prayed especially in the morning, again at noontime, in the late afternoon, and finally just before going to sleep.

Whatever your approach to prayer, there are prayers in this section that I trust you will be comfortable using during your time alone with God. Besides the formal prayers (which follow the general pattern of "official" prayers of many denominations), there are shorter, informal prayers as well as specific prayers both for times of turmoil and for times of joy and thankfulness.

Do you find yourself feeling too rushed to pray at noon or later in the day? This is not unusual, but the busyness that causes us to skip prayer time may be all the more reason to pray. Sharing a few thoughts with God might be the very thing needed to get us through a busy afternoon. If you have to face the demands of children at home, the pressure of a business meeting, the need to study, or any of a hundred other stressful activities, *take time for prayer on a regular basis.* Take time at noon and later in the afternoon as well. Pray just before the kids come home from school or at the end of your coffee break. Pray while you are headed home after work, or right after dinner and before beginning your evening activities. Pick a time that will be available on an average day, and make praying at that time as much of a habit as eating.

If your prayer life has become lax, make a commitment during one of your alone-with-God sessions to get back in the prayer habit. Pray morning, midday, afternoon, and end of the day prayers regularly *for three weeks.* At the end of that time, you are likely to find the discipline becoming natural for you.

IN THE MORNING
Introduction (Psalm 134:1)
Come, bless Yahweh, all you who serve Yahweh.

Psalm 111
Alleluia! I will thank you, Yahweh, with all my heart
in the meeting of the just and their assembly.
Great are your works
to be pondered by all who love them.
Glorious and sublime are your works;
your justice stands firm forever.
You help us remember your wonders.
You are compassion and love.
You give food to those who fear you,
keeping your covenant ever in mind.
You have shown your might to your people
by giving them the lands of the nations.
Your works are justice and truth;
your precepts are all of them sure;
they are steadfast forever and ever,
made in uprightness and faithfulness.
You have sent deliverance to your people
and established your covenant forever.
Holy your name, greatly to be feared.*
To fear** you is the beginning of wisdom;
all who do so prove themselves wise.
Your praise shall last forever!

114

*Our English version may make it difficult for us to understand the richness of meaning the psalmist is attempting to convey. The writer wants us to realize that the very name of the Lord ought to fill us with a combination of wonder, awe, respect, and love.
**We might better understand "fear" to be "respect-filled love."

Response
For my life, I praise you, loving Creator.
For the newly created day and opportunity, I praise you, loving Creator.
For all the people who love me, and all those who find it hard to love me, I praise you, loving Creator.
For Jesus Christ, I praise you, loving Creator.

Scripture Reading
"Then, turning to the disciples Jesus said to them privately, 'Blessed are the eyes that see what you see! For I tell you that many prophets and kings desired to see what you see, and did not see it, and to hear what you hear, but did not hear it'" (Luke 10:23-24).

Prayer
O God, you are the mighty creator and sustainer of the world. You placed me in the midst of your creation that I might see your goodness and praise your mighty works. Grant me the insight to continue to foster the right use and protection of the earth, that all may be brought into the fullness of the light of the world, Jesus. Amen.

Silent Time for Personal Intercessions
The Lord's Prayer

Blessing
May the God who placed me in the midst of this creation fill me with the powerful Spirit. *Amen.*

MIDDAY PRAYER

Introduction

As the sun is high in the sky, may I stand in the brightness of your light, O God.

Psalm 67

God, show your faithfulness, bless us,
and make your face smile on us!
For then the earth will acknowledge your ways,
and all the nations will know of your power to save.
May all the nations praise you, O God;
may all the nations praise you!
Let the nations shout and sing for joy
since you dispense true justice to the world.
You grant strict justice to the peoples;
on earth you guide the nations.
Let the nations praise you, God;
let all the nations praise you!
The soil has given its harvest;
God, our God, has blessed us.
May God continue to bless us;
and let God be feared to the very ends of the earth.

Prayer

I acclaim you, gracious God, for all your mighty gifts. You provide me with bread and drink day by day. You cover me with your wings of protection within my home. Open my eyes to see more clearly your power in our midst, that all those I know may come to an ever greater understanding of your love. Grant that as I come to appreciate your love more and more, I may be a reminder for others that you are gracious to your people. I pray in Jesus' name. *Amen.*

Scripture Reading

"Therefore I tell you, do not worry about your life, what you will eat or what you will drink, or about your body, what you will wear. Is not life more than food, and the body more than clothing? Look at the birds of the air; they neither sow nor reap nor gather into barns, and yet your heavenly Father feeds them. Are you not of more value than they?" (Matthew 6:25-26).

Silence for Reflecting on How The Word Relates to Your Life

Intercessions

For all who are homeless, I pray in trust, O Provider.
For all who are hungry, I pray in trust, O Provider.
For all who are at war, I pray in trust, O Provider.
For all who seek truth and justice, I pray in trust, O Provider.
For all people whose lives I touch, I pray in trust, O Provider.

The Lord's Prayer

Blessing

As God makes the sun to shine on the earth, may God's face shine upon me. *Amen.*

EVENING PRAYER

Introduction

At the setting of the sun, may God be blessed!

Psalm 113

Alleluia!
Praise, you servants of Yahweh,
praise the name of Yahweh!
May Yahweh's name be blessed
both now and forever!
From east to west, from north to south,
praised be the name of Yahweh!
High above all nations, Yahweh!
Your glory transcends the heavens!
Who is like you, Yahweh our God?
Enthroned so high, you have to stoop
to see the heavens and earth!
You raise the poor from the dust
and lift the needy from the dunghill
to give them a place with rulers,
with the nobles of your people.
Yahweh, you give the barren a home,
making them glad with children.

Response

For all the times I have been forgiven, may God be blessed.
For my friends and family, may God be blessed.
For the times I have felt God's presence, may God be blessed.
For this time of prayer, may God be blessed.

Scripture Reading

"Again, the kingdom of heaven is like a net that was thrown into the sea and caught fish of every kind; when it was full, they drew it ashore, sat down, and put the good into baskets but threw out the bad" (Matthew 13:47-48).

Prayer

God, as I come to the evening of this day, grant that I may see more clearly all the aspects of my life, those for which I give thanks and those for which I ask forgiveness. Lead me to a greater under-standing of the importance of decisions I make each day. Grant that I may be a symbol of the kingdom of heaven to those people I already know and those I am about to meet. *Amen.*

Silent Time for Personal Intercessions
The Lord's Prayer

Blessing

May the Spirit that filled this day with life and new opportunities continue to fill this evening and night with the power of God's love. *Amen.*

PRAYER AT DAY'S END
Introduction
Blessed be the God of the heavens, of the sun and of the moon.

Psalm 134
Come, bless Yahweh,
all you who serve Yahweh,
ministering in the house of Yahweh,
in the courts of the house of our God!
Lift up your hands toward the sanctuary;
praise Yahweh night after night!
May Yahweh bless you from Zion,
the One who made heaven and earth!

Silence for Intercessions

Scripture Reading
Now may the God of peace, who brought back from the dead our
Lord Jesus, the great shepherd of the sheep, by the blood of the
eternal covenant, make you complete in everything good so that you
may do his will, working among us that which is pleasing in his
sight, through Jesus Christ, to whom be the glory forever and ever.
Amen (Hebrews 13:20-21).

Silence for Confession of Your Faults of This Day

Prayer
"Master, now you are dismissing your servant in peace, according to
your word; for my eyes have seen your salvation, which you have
prepared in the presence of all peoples, a light for revelation to the
Gentiles and for glory to your people Israel" (Luke 2:29-32).

Blessing
May God grant me a peaceful night, and give strength to those who
work while I sleep. *Amen.*

MORNING PRAYER

God, at the beginning of this new day
I give thanks to you with my whole heart.
For my life . . . I praise you.
For the newly created day
and the opportunity it may bring . . . I praise you.
For all my friends . . . I praise you.
Grant me patience and understanding, and
may your ever-present love be felt by those I know.
Today, I ask especially that you bless
(my spouse, friend, boss, child, neighbor). *Amen.*

MIDDAY PRAYER

In the middle of this busy day,
I turn to you, God, with hope in my heart.
I look at the birds of the air, who neither sow nor reap,
and try to understand that you care for them
and you care for me.
Caring God, I am grateful for all my blessings,
but I continue to need your help.
Open my eyes so that I see more clearly
how your love may come to life through me
as I go about my work this afternoon. *Amen.*

EVENING PRAYER

O God, it has been a busy day
and I need to feel your comforting presence.
Refresh me,
so that I might be patient with those I love. *Amen.*

PRAYER AT DAY'S END

Now, at the end of my day,
I place my trust in you, ever present God.
Be present to all those people
who are important to me, especially (names).
Forgive me for whatever hurts I have caused,
strengthen the belief that lies within my heart,
and grant me a restful sleep. *Amen.*

PRAYER FOR FORGIVENESS
God of all creation, I ask pardon for my faults,
for all the times when I have done or thought
or said things harmful to myself or others.
I regret those times when through negligence
I did not do, think, or say what would have helped.
Forgive me as I forgive others who have harmed me.
I ask to be forgiven in Jesus' name. *Amen.*

PRAYER OF PRAISE TO GOD
For all those who love me, I praise you, God.
For this time alone, I praise you.
For all those who have been my teachers, I praise you.
For the beauty of sun and sky, I praise you.
For my mind and all it can do, I praise you.
For life and love, I praise you. *Amen.*

PRAYER OF GRIEF
Dear God, death is so hard to accept.
I feel anger, pain.
I feel numb, empty.
I do not sleep well, I do not eat well.
Dear God, death is so hard to understand.
I feel no joy, no hope.
I only feel love lost.
Dear God, help me survive the pain of loss.
I pray in Jesus' name. *Amen.*

PRAYER FOR PATIENCE
I know that being patient is not one of my strengths.
Everyone who knows me knows that.
Today, I don't even have the patience to pray!
God, please help me to sit quietly,
breathe deeply, and be patient. *Amen.*

PRAYER OF HOPE

O God, I have a song to sing.
Help me sing it.
I have a dream to make real.
Help me to do it.
I have myself to be.
Help me to be all that I can be.
And if I stop singing or forget my dreams,
help me to begin again with hope. *Amen.*

PRAYER FOR BELIEF

God of wind and setting sun,
God of babies crying and kids playing,
God of my best dreams,
I want to believe.
I want my belief to be something
that encourages me to grow.
I want my belief to be something
that guides me toward finding meaning in life.
I seek a faith to free me to live, not just exist.
Dear God, this is my prayer: Help me to believe. *Amen.*

PRAYER FOR THE SICK

God, Creator of life,
you know I don't handle sickness very well.
Help those who, like me, are sick of being sick.
Inspire nurses and doctors to have compassion,
and to take time to listen to patients
who need a friendly word as much as medicine.
Guide visitors to the bedridden at home who feel forgotten.
Bestow patience on anyone who suffers alone.
Help me to be faithful to my beliefs
in times of sickness as well as times of health.
I pray in the name of Jesus,
who suffered and died that we might live. *Amen.*

PRAYER FOR THE DIVORCED
God, will I ever understand?
I believed in marriage, gave to it what I could.
Still, it has ended. And there is pain. And anger. And fear.
There has never been a time in my life
when I felt such a need for someone to love me.
Please, take away my sense of failure.
Please, let me sense your presence in my life,
and help me to feel worthy once again. *Amen.*

PRAYER FOR FAMILIES
Dear God, I pray that you watch over and protect all families.
I pray especially for troubled families.
Where there is abuse, bring change.
Where there is infidelity, restore faithful love.
Where there is yelling, inspire calm.
Where there is alienation, reunite people.
Make us all more sensitive to one another's needs
so that we may reach out in love
to create strong families and wise people. *Amen.*

PSALM 4
Answer me when I call, God, my defender!
When I was in trouble, you came to my help.
Be kind to me now; hear my prayer!
How long will you people insult me?
How long will you love what is worthless
and seek what is false?
Remember that Yahweh has chosen me and hears me when I call.
Tremble, and stop your sinning;
think deeply about this, alone and silent in your rooms.
Offer the right sacrifices to the Holy One
and put your trust in God.
There are many who say, "How we wish to receive a blessing!"
Look on us with kindness, Yahweh!
The joy that you give me is much greater
than the joy of those who have an abundance of grain and wine.
As soon as I lie down, I peacefully go to sleep;
you alone, my Strength, keep me perfectly safe.

PSALM 46

God is our refuge and our strength,
our ever-present help in distress.
Though the earth trembles,
and mountains slide into the sea,
we have no fear.
Waters foam and roar,
and mountains shake at their surging;
but the God of hosts is with us—
our stronghold, the God of Israel.
There is a river
whose streams give joy to the city of God,
the holy dwelling of the Most High.
God is in its midst; it stands firm.
God will aid it at the break of day.
Even if nations are in chaos, and kingdoms fall,
God's voice resounds; the earth melts away.
Yahweh is with us;
the God of Israel is our stronghold.
Come! See the deeds of the Most High,
the marvelous things God has done on earth;
all over the world, God has stopped wars—
breaking bows, splintering spears,
burning the shields with fire.
"Be still! and know that I am God,
exalted among the nations, exalted upon the earth."
The Most High is with us;
our stronghold is the God of Israel.

PSALM 61

Hear my cry, O God; listen to my prayer.
From the end of the earth
I call to you with fainting heart.
Lift me up and set me high upon a rock.
For you have been my shelter,
a tower of strength against the enemy.
In your tent will I make my home forever
and find my refuge under the shelter of your wings.
For you, O God, have accepted my vows

and granted me the heritage of all who honor your name.
To the leader's life add length of days,
year upon year for many generations.
The ruler may dwell in God's presence forever,
preserved by true and faithful love.
So will I ever sing psalms in praise of your name
as I fulfill my vows day after day.

PSALM 121
I lift my eyes to the mountains.
Where is help to come from?
My help comes from Yahweh,
who made heaven and earth.
Yahweh does not let our footsteps slip!
Our guard does not sleep!
The guardian of Israel
does not slumber or sleep.
Yahweh guards you, shades you.
With Yahweh at your right hand
the sun cannot harm you by day
nor the moon at night.
Yahweh guards you from harm,
protects your lives;
Yahweh watches over your coming and going,
now and for always.

A F T E R W O R D

Never Really Alone

✳

A time comes when your retreat must end. Whether you have been alone with God for two hours or two days, something unusual has happened: God's Spirit has breathed on you. Perhaps some doors that were closed have opened to reveal not only a need to change but a way to change. You may have felt the wondrous release of being forgiven or sensed a peacefulness you would like to hold onto forever.

At all the retreats I have had the privilege to take part in, there is a moment when the participants gather just before leaving and inevitably someone says, "Well, it's time to go back to the real world." There seems to be an unspoken consensus that God is active only in our quiet, alone times.

Wherever you end your own retreat, be thankful for the quiet time, but do not leave feeling that the *real* times of prayer are when you are alone behind a closed door, isolated in the woods, or sitting alone in a chapel. Such moments are spiritually rich because we are freed of distractions. It is not unusual under such circumstances to become so committed to being alone with God that we think God is alone with us. This place where we have had such a good experience is certainly not the only place where God is active. And despite the feelings we may have had, we are not God's only partners. God is God of the universe and beyond. God is God of all—those we love and those we do not love.

126

Although we are invited to take our time alone with God in a retreat setting and be strengthened by the experience, we must also be in the world as Jesus was and be aware that God is present at *all* times and in *all* places. Few of us are born to be hermits who could, or should, live in prayerful isolation. Most of us are called to listen, touch other lives, and heal within our own communities. As people of faith we are nourished by retreats and thus better prepared to proclaim peace and justice.

We are called to proclaim the same Spirit of God as Jesus did when he began his ministry. In a Nazareth synagogue on a Sabbath day, Jesus read these words aloud from the book of the prophet Isaiah:

"The Spirit of the Lord is upon me, because he has anointed me to bring good news to the poor. He has sent me to proclaim release to the captives and recovery of sight to the blind, to let the oppressed go free, to proclaim the year of the Lord's favor" (Luke 4:18-19).

The direction of a personal ministry, which we touched on in Session 10, "Called to Serve," may remain the same or change from year to year and even from month to month. By taking alonetime, you not only praise and glorify God, but also have the opportunity to reflect on how you are being nourished by the gift of God's love and what that gift is preparing you to do.

Through your experience of alonetime, you have been prepared to live life more abundantly. So go forth, ready to respond with love to the people closest to you, the people with whom you live and work and play. These are the people with whom you and I must continue planting the seeds of peace and justice that we would like to see grow around the world.

Go forth, rejoicing in the power of the Holy Spirit!